'Although Karl Rahner is cc
twentieth-century theologian
the whole point of his theology is to bring out the unity and simplicity of Christian faith. In this beautifully lucid and sympathetic study, she has managed marvellously to render the character and key elements of his thought accessible to the general reader.'

Nicholas Lash
Professor Emeritus of Divinity
University of Cambridge

'Lucid, perceptive, thickly textured, theologically rich, and refreshingly concise – Kilby's presentation of Rahner's theology is a must for students of Rahner, be they first-year seminarians or senior theologians. I have taught her book for years and I still learn something new from it every time I return – it's brilliant reading.'

Serene Jones
Yale Divinity School

'Karen Kilby's book will be invaluable to teachers and students because of its lucid, learned and penetrating understanding of one of the most important theologians of the twentieth century. It is the best single slim volume on Rahner that I know.'

Gavin D'Costa
University of Bristol

'Karen Kilby's book is an imaginative, clear and succinct work. It offers many illustrative and accessible analogies which I have found invaluable in communicating important aspects of Rahner's thought to students.'

Philip Caldwell
Ushaw College, Durham

'Lucidly argued and accessibly written . . . newcomers are well advised to read this book first . . . [a] finely judged introduction.'

Fergus Kerr
Reviews in Religion and Theology

'I have never come across a more useful tool in presenting Rahner to undergraduates than Kilby's book. It is a model of succinctness and precision, but far more importantly, it succeeds in accurately identifying and unpacking the key to Rahner's thought in a very reader-friendly way.'

Eamonn Mulcahy
Missionary Institute, London

'This is an excellent book, very useful for students and one of the clearest introductions to Rahner.'

John McDade
Principal of Heythrop College, London

Karen Kilby is an Associate Professor in the Department of Theology and Religious Studies at the University of Nottingham, and is on the staff of its Centre of Theology and Philosophy. She is the author of *Karl Rahner: Theology and Philosophy* (Routledge, 2004), and is currently engaged in writing *Von Balthasar: A Very Critical Introduction* for Eerdmans.

KARL RAHNER

A Brief Introduction

Karen Kilby

A Herder & Herder Book
The Crossroad Publishing Company
New York

First published in Great Britain in 1997 as *Karl Rahner*
by Fount Paperbacks, an imprint of HarperCollins Publishers

This edition published in the United States of America in 2007

The Crossroad Publishing Company
16 Penn Plaza
New York, NY 10001

Printed in Great Britain.

Library of Congress Cataloging-in-Publication data is available.

ISBN 10: 0–8245–2428–4
ISBN 13: 978–0–8245–2428–9

1 2 3 4 5 6 7 8 9 10   12 11 10 09 08 07

Contents

Acknowledgements

This book is a revised and significantly expanded version of an introduction to the thought of Karl Rahner first published in the Fount Christian Thinkers series, edited by Peter Vardy. The whole text has been revised, and the chapters on philosophy and on spirituality are entirely new. I am very grateful to Peter Vardy for encouraging me to write the original book, and to Rebecca Mulhearn of SPCK for her support and patience in the process of revising and expanding it. My thanks go also to Steve Gove, whose careful copy-editing has saved me from some at least of the dangers inherent in adding to a book a number of years after it was originally written, and finally, to George Lindbeck, in whose seminars I first became confused by Rahner.

The book is dedicated to my uncle, Werner Baer, in gratitude for his encouragement over many years.

Abbreviations

CS   *Church and the Sacraments, The*, tr. W. J. O'Hara (London: Burns & Oates, 1974)

ES   *Encounters with Silence*, tr. James M. Demske (South Bend, St Augustine's Press, 1999)

FCF   *Foundations of Christian Faith: An Introduction to the Idea of Christianity*, tr. William Dych (London: Darton, Longman & Todd, 1978)

IR   *I Remember*, tr. Harvey D. Egan, SJ (London: SCM Press, 1985)

KRD   *Karl Rahner in Dialogue*, ed. Paul Inhot and Albert Biallowons, various trs (New York: Crossroad, 1986)

OH   *On Heresy*, tr. W. J. O'Hara (London: Burns & Oates, 1964)

PF   *Practice of Faith, The: A Handbook of Contemporary Spirituality*, ed. Karl Lehmann and Albert Raffelt (New York: Crossroad, 1983)

SE   *Spiritual Exercises*, tr. Kenneth Baker, SJ (London: Sheed & Ward, 1967)

SW   *Spirit in the World*, tr. William Dych (London: Herder & Herder, 1979)

TI   *Theological Investigations* (23 volumes), various trs (I–VI, Baltimore: Helicon, 1961–9; VII–X, New York: Herder & Herder, 1970–3; XI–XIV, New York: Seebury, 1974–6; XV–XXI, New York: Crossroad, 1979–88; XXII–XXIII, London: Darton, Longman & Todd, 1991–2)

Date chart

1904   Born in Freiburg in Breisgau, West Germany
1922   Finishes secondary school
       Enters the Society of Jesus (Jesuits)
1932   Ordained a priest
1934–6 Undertakes doctoral studies in philosophy; attends
       seminars of Martin Heidegger
1936   Undertakes doctoral studies in theology
1937   Begins teaching theology
1939   Failed philosophy Ph.D. thesis published under title
       Spirit in the World
1941   *Hearer of the Word* published
1951   Prevented from publishing a book on the Assump-
       tion of Mary
1954   First volume of *Theological Investigations* published
1962   Told that all his work will have to be read in advance
       by a Roman censor. Becomes 'peritus', theological
       expert, at the Second Vatican Council
1971   Retires from teaching
1976   *Foundations of Christian Faith* published
1984   Dies in Innsbruck, Austria

Introduction

Karl Rahner was born in 1904 into a reasonably pious, reasonably middle-class German Catholic family. At the age of 18 he entered the Society of Jesus, and he remained a Jesuit all his life. He was trained, he was ordained, he earned a doctorate, he taught, he wrote, he retired, he wrote some more, and, in 1984, he died. He did not do anything special in World War II. He could not in old age remember quite what his motives were for becoming a Jesuit – just the usual ones a young man would have, he supposed. He had no great hobbies, underwent no shattering conversion experiences, held no high offices. Altogether a rather boring life.

But look again, and it gets a little more interesting. Rahner was born into one kind of Catholic Church, and he died in a rather different one, and he himself, his own writing and lecturing, had a good deal to do with the change. In the 1950s he was on the margins, his orthodoxy questioned, his work censored; in the 1960s, suddenly, he was at the centre of things, a theological expert at the Second Vatican Council, and, in almost all accounts but his own, one of the shaping influences upon it.

Rahner has to be counted not only among the most influential, but also among the most intriguing thinkers in modern theology. He is a figure in whom opposites, or apparent opposites, meet in an unusual way. He combines a profound immersion in the Christian tradition, for instance, with a conviction that theology needs to be thoroughly modern. He puts experience at the centre of his thought, and yet believes in the importance of dogma. He accepts the teaching authority of the Roman Catholic Church, with all the constraints this can impose, but writes with great freedom and creativity. The paradoxes can be multiplied. Rahner is considered one of the most dense and difficult of twentieth-century theologians, but he believes that the whole point of his theology is to bring out the utter unity and simplicity of the Christian faith. He is a powerfully systematic thinker, yet writes hundreds and thousands of short, dispersed essays and describes himself as a theological 'dilettante', a dabbler.

Rahner's efforts to reconcile tradition and modernity, dogma and experience, freedom and authority, are not always equally successful. Sometimes the result is brilliant; sometimes it is tortuous or simply unconvincing. Few readers will want to follow Rahner at every point, and many find him at times irritating. And yet one cannot come to grips with Rahner's thought without recognizing oneself to be in the presence of an unusually broad and powerful mind. If Rahner can be unpersuasive and even irritating on occasion, he can also open up new and intriguing ways of looking at Christian belief, and suggest new and fascinating ways of thinking about our experience.

To make sense of Rahner's thought it is helpful to have some knowledge of the context within which he worked. At the time Rahner received his basic philosophical and theological training, the Catholic intellectual world was dominated by a single, comprehensive system of thought. This had not always been so. In the first part of the nineteenth century a number of ways of doing theology, drawing on very different styles of philosophy, had existed side by side. But during the second half of the century one school of thought managed to defeat all the others and establish itself as *the* Catholic philosophy and theology. As is often the case, it presented itself not as something new but as a return to an earlier, golden era, namely the era of 'scholasticism', the Middle Ages. Neo-scholasticism, as this school of thought came to be known, based itself more particularly on the philosophical and theological system of Thomas Aquinas (1225–74) – or rather, Aquinas as interpreted by Catholic theologians of the sixteenth and seventeenth centuries. And this is the system into which Rahner, together with all other men preparing for the priesthood in the first half of the twentieth century, was trained.

Neo-scholasticism was both a satisfying and a frustrating intellectual system – and both for the same reasons. It was a highly structured, self-enclosed system, one which had turned its back on the modern world and all the intellectual difficulties it raises. It offered a world which was orderly and in which everything had its place. Certain questions were open for debate and disagreement and differing opinion, but these were definite, circumscribed questions, contained within a much larger whole where everything was worked out and all the important matters already resolved.

Much of Rahner's work, particularly his work before the 1960s[1] and the Second Vatican Council, can be understood as an effort to open up this neo-scholasticism. This means that he neither accepted the state of Roman Catholic thought as it was, nor simply turned his back on it, but tried to change it from within. Again and again he tried to show that everything was not so neatly tied up as it seemed in this system, that there was scope for new ideas, a need for new thinking, and room for engagement with the modern world.

Rahner's approach to Aquinas was typical of this. He neither denied nor questioned the importance of St Thomas – to do so would have been to put himself right outside the boundaries of neo-scholasticism. But he *interpreted* Aquinas in a radically different way from most neo-scholastics.[2] He wrote about Aquinas with language borrowed from the twentieth-century philosopher Martin Heidegger, and he believed that one could find in Aquinas many of the questions and issues raised by Immanuel Kant, the most important philosopher of modernity. So an allegiance to Aquinas did not have to involve a refusal to come to terms with more recent developments: being faithful to Aquinas, as Rahner presented it, was fully compatible with living in the contemporary world and engaging with modern thought.

One way to describe Rahner's work, then, is as an effort to open up the closed world of neo-scholasticism. It must immediately be added, however, that this is only one way to describe it, and that no one phrase can summarize what Rahner was up to. It could equally be said that Rahner developed a 'transcendental theology', or that he constructed a theology of experience, or that everything he wrote was centred upon the conviction that God is 'absolute mystery'. Rahner's thought is rich and many-layered and not easily caught by any particular account of it. His writings, like the writings of most important thinkers, can be approached in a variety of ways, and appreciated (or criticized) on many different levels.

This introduction is necessarily selective. It does not pretend to offer a comprehensive overview of Rahner's philosophy and theology. Instead it sketches a few of the central themes of Rahner's thought, and tries to give the reader some feeling for the way he approaches problems and some sense of the breadth of his work.

1

God and humanity

Rahner produced one of the most difficult philosophical works of the twentieth century in his youth, *Spirit in the World* (SW).[1] During the more than forty years that followed he kept up a tremendous intellectual output, right through to the distilled, simplified and sometimes crotchety reflections of an old man. Over the decades it is possible to detect a variety of changes – changes in his positions and changes in his interests, changes in style, tone and emphasis. But one thing which remains constant, which comes up again and again through the whole span of Rahner's writings, is a distinctive conception of what it is that makes us human, a distinctive *picture* of the human being. Sometimes Rahner tries (with questionable success) to give a strict philosophical argument for key elements in this picture, a proof from first principles. Sometimes he tries to evoke in the reader a recognition of what he is talking about, to make his audience say, 'Yes, maybe my experience really is something like that.' Sometimes – most often, in fact – he simply uses the picture, shows that other things begin to fall into place if we consider human beings in this light.

Rahner's conception of what it is to be human is by no means an obvious or a common-sense one. It is not what one would hear if one were to ask the man in the street what he understands himself to be. At first sight it is not even, perhaps, particularly plausible. But it is well worth trying to come to grips with this picture, both because it offers an unusual perspective from which to think about ourselves and our experience, and because it is so often crucial for understanding what Rahner is up to.

What is both strange and powerful about Rahner's picture of the human being is, to put it very simply, the way in which God comes into it. Being related to God is absolutely fundamental, on Rahner's account, to who and what we are. Now this may at first sound neither strange nor powerful but like something of a platitude. Any self-respecting theologian, indeed any priest or minister or pious Christian, is going to tell us that God is important for human beings. But what Rahner is getting at here is something rather different from the ordinary pieties. It is not just that we may or may not (but should) think about God, pray to God, live good lives and be with God in heaven after we die. It is not just that God, 'in the beginning', created us along with everything else, or even that God constantly sustains us, together with the rest of creation, in being. It is not just that we ought perhaps to try to develop a relationship with God. On Rahner's account we are, whether we realize it or not, *already* related to God. Furthermore, this relatedness is absolutely essential to us. It is so deeply built into us, so absolutely critical in making us what we are, that nothing we do would be possible without it. Being related to God is so much a part of our structure, if Rahner is to be believed, that it is not possible properly to describe what it is to love, or what it is to will or even to think, in the perfectly ordinary, human way, without bringing God into the description.

Rahner develops this rather extraordinary claim in the most detail in connection with knowing. He begins with what he takes to be the most basic and simple kind of knowing, when a person recognizes something for what it is and forms a judgement such as 'This is a chair.' In every such basic intellectual act, Rahner maintains, in every act of knowing a particular, limited object in the world, the knower also has a certain awareness of the unlimited, of 'infinite Being', and with this, of God.

If one wanted to do a proper philosophical analysis of Rahner's position one would need to look very carefully at the two very bold steps he is taking here. One would want to know, first, how he tries to show that knowledge of a particular, finite being automatically brings with it awareness of 'infinite Being' (whatever that might be), and secondly, how he gets from this infinite Being to God. I will say a little bit more about these questions, particularly the first, in Chapter 5, but for the moment our aim is not to examine philosophical arguments but simply to try to get some feeling for the picture Rahner is working towards, for his basic vision of how God enters into all our most ordinary human knowing. And so we will ignore for the moment the question of how Rahner thinks he can establish the claims he makes, and try to understand simply what it is that he is claiming. What can it in fact mean to say that all people, even secular, non-mystical people, even atheists indeed, have this constant awareness of God?

I have already been taking a certain liberty, because Rahner himself does not speak precisely of an 'awareness' of God. He uses a technical term (*Vorgriff*) and there is a certain amount of debate about how it should be translated into English ('pre-apprehension' and 'anticipation' seem to be the two leading contenders). Luckily, however, it is perfectly possible to ignore the term itself, whether in German or in English, and concentrate instead on the various *images* Rahner relies on, images of how this awareness (or whatever it is) of God is related to our knowing of particular items in the world. It is from these images, and in particular images of movement, of light, and of the horizon, that one can get some feeling for what he is after.

There is first of all, then, an image of movement. Rahner describes the mind as *reaching out* beyond any given object, any particular item in the world – a chair or a table – towards infinite being and therefore God. Furthermore, he says, it is only in the process of this reaching out that the particular object can be grasped in the first place. The mind has a *dynamism*, a fundamental drive, beyond any and every finite object towards the infinity of being and God, and this dynamism is a 'condition of the possibility' of knowledge – without such a drive towards the infinite the finite could not be known.

To get some purchase on this idea it might be helpful to consider the process of climbing a mountain. Imagine Edmund Hillary working his way up Mount Everest. On the one hand Hillary moves towards the peak; on the other hand he takes particular steps. The two things are of course inseparable: Hillary takes steps because of the desire to get to the top, and the movement towards the summit happens only *in* his steps. Now suppose that Mount Everest is in fact *infinitely* high, so that though each step is a movement towards the peak, nevertheless with each step Hillary remains at the same infinite distance from it. Then it would be possible to say something similar to what Rahner wants to say: in every finite act, with every step, there is a dynamism, a fundamental drive, *towards* the infinite goal, and on the other hand it is only *because* of the infinite goal, only because Hillary's eyes are set on the top, that the finite acts, the individual steps, can take place. Just as moving towards the mountain's peak is not something that occurs *in addition* to putting one foot in front of the other, so the mind's dynamism towards infinite being and God always takes place *in* the act of knowing particular objects in the world. And just as it is the basic desire to get to the top that makes the climber take individual steps, so it is that Rahner says that the mind's basic dynamism towards God is what makes possible its knowledge of finite objects.

At certain points this analogy breaks down. Climbers are usually set on getting to the top in a very *explicit*, fully conscious way. If you had asked Edmund Hillary what he was doing he would have told you in no uncertain terms. The same cannot be said of our dynamism towards God: this takes place on such a deep level, by Rahner's account, that though it shapes and indeed makes possible all that we do, we may not be explicitly conscious of it. In fact it is impossible ever to be fully reflectively aware of it.

Another problem with the analogy is that it suggests a kind of *progress* – step by step the climber moves ever higher – and this is not part of what Rahner is trying to put across with his talk of movement and dynamism. He is telling us about what he takes to be the basic structure of *any* of our acts, and not about something that accumulates over a lifetime.

A second, more straightforward image that Rahner sometimes uses to point to the relationship between our awareness of God and our knowledge of everyday things is that of *light*. We need light to see, and when we look at a book, say, we also at the same time have a certain awareness of the light which allows us to see it. Our awareness of infinite being and of God can be thought of along the lines of a light which, in illuminating particular objects, makes them knowable. As light enables us to see, so the awareness of God, the mind's reaching out towards God, enables us to know. And just as we do not see the light in the same way as we see the book – the book is what we see, the light is that *by which* we see – so though we have a kind of awareness of God, we never have a knowledge of God akin to our knowledge of objects.

Rahner's favourite image, the image to which he returns most frequently, is that of a horizon. We always know particular objects against and within the infinite horizon of Being and therefore of God. One might equally use the language of foreground and background here. Particular finite objects, chairs and tables and eggs, are in the foreground of our knowing, but in the background, the background which can itself never *become* the foreground, is our awareness of infinite Being and of God.

So with this notion of the *Vorgriff*, however we want to translate it, Rahner is trying to suggest that all our knowledge of things in the world is both accompanied by and made possible by some sort of awareness of that which goes beyond the world, of God. But he is not content just to say this. It is not only in our knowing, but in everything we do, that on some level we are dealing with God. It is not only when we know, but also when we will, when we make a choice and exercise our freedom, that we have a dynamism towards God, and even an experience of God. When we choose any finite object our will is always at the same time going beyond it towards the infinite good, which is God.

What about if what we choose to do is to murder, rape and pillage? Do we still have an experience of God? Is our will even then moving towards God? Rahner's answer would be, quite simply, yes. Freedom, whether it is used for good or ill, simply could not exist without this relatedness to God. We may choose to act in ways that are utterly contradictory with the fact that we are directed towards God, but our very ability to choose comes from this directedness.

In every dimension of our existence, then, the same pattern occurs: we are always dealing with God, but always indirectly,[2] always *in* our dealings with that which is not God, with the world. Rahner returns again and again to this basic idea. It is both a very simple idea and an extraordinarily elusive one, and so he circles round and round it, looking for new ways to express it. Sometimes, for instance, he talks about our relationship to God as an orientation towards *mystery*, or towards *holy mystery*:

Whether he is consciously aware of it or not, whether he is open to this truth or suppresses it, man's whole spiritual and intellectual existence is orientated towards a holy mystery which is the basis of his being. This mystery is the inexplicit and unexpressed horizon which always encircles and upholds the small area of our every-day experience of knowing and acting, our knowledge of reality and our free action. It is our most fundamental, most natural condition, but for that very reason it is also the most hidden and least regarded reality, speaking to us by its silence, and even whilst appearing to be absent, revealing its presence by making us take cognizance of our own limitations. (TI IX 122)

Mystery, as Rahner wants to use the word, is that which we cannot control, that which we cannot grasp or comprehend or define or manipulate. But mystery in this sense is not just something that meets us at the *edge* of our knowledge. It is not a mystery which, if we only had a bit more information, or a new insight, we could *solve*. It is not just that as yet there remain gaps in what we can know and control. Mystery, as Rahner thinks it should be understood, is much more fundamental, more all-pervasive in our lives:

> Man is he who is always confronted with the holy mystery, even where he is dealing with what is within hand's reach, comprehensible and amenable to a conceptual framework . . . the holy mystery is not something upon which man may 'also' stumble, if he is lucky and takes an interest in something else besides the definable objects within the horizon of his consciousness. Man always lives by the holy mystery, even where he is not conscious of it. (TI IV 54)

And it is because we thus live in the presence of mystery, in Rahner's view, that we can interact with the non-mysterious, that we can know, control and manipulate finite objects:

> Man always lives by the holy mystery, even where he is not conscious of it. The lucidity of his consciousness derives from the incomprehensibility of this mystery. The proximity of his environment is constituted by the distant aloofness of the mystery: the freedom of his mastery of things comes from his being mastered by the Holy which is itself unmastered. (TI IV 54)

Most great Christian theologians have a certain love of paradox, and as these passages make clear, Rahner is no exception.

But his talk of mystery does more than provide the opportunity for revelling in paradoxical language. It is intended to make the reader attend to a certain dimension of experience afresh, in a new way, in a way that the over-used language of 'God' might not. And it is also intended to stop short any tendency we may have to imagine that 'God' is an easy word to understand, just another concept that we can pin down, one thing among many others that we can talk about with equal facility.

Another, rather more technical, way in which Rahner often formulates his basic vision of human beings is by means of an opposition between *transcendental* and *categorical* experience. Strictly speaking these are not two different experiences but two different dimensions of all our experiencing. We have only one, unified experience, but it has two sides to it. Categorical experience is our experience in so far as it involves us with the finite, with particular real people or objects, with things that can be put into categories, with things to which we can apply concepts, of which we can use language. To transcend means simply 'to go beyond', and so our transcendental experience is the experience we have of going beyond all the things which we know and choose and love, even as we are knowing and choosing and loving them: transcendental experience, in Rahner's words, is the experience which 'consists precisely in the transcendence beyond any particular group of possible objects or of categories'. And since when we go beyond all the things of this world what we go *towards* is God, transcendental experience turns out to be, most fundamentally, the experience we have of God in all our ordinary experience.

Though transcendental and categorical experiences can be distinguished, they cannot be separated. Rahner insists that transcendental experience does not occur *apart from* categorical experience – we do not have an experience of God neat, all on its own, but always only *in* our experiencing of the concrete, categorical realities. Transcendental experience is not, however, just an *accompaniment* to categorical experience, a kind of added bonus. It does more than just make our ordinary experience a little bit richer. According to Rahner it makes our ordinary experience possible in the first place. Transcendental experience, Rahner maintains, is a *condition of the possibility* of categorical experience, that without which we would not be able to have any experience at all.

There is another, and very important, way in which the two layers in our experience are related. Transcendental experience, Rahner maintains, always needs in some way to *articulate itself*, to express itself, in categorical experience. By definition, of course, transcendental experience is that realm of experience where language fails, since we have language for objects, for distinguishing one thing from another, but not for that which in principle cannot be an object, not for the infinite horizon within which all this distinguishing takes place:

> The horizon cannot be comprised within the horizon . . .
> The ultimate measure cannot be measured; the boundary
> which delimits all things cannot itself be bounded by a still
> more distant limit . . . (TI IV 51)

And yet, in spite of all this, transcendental experience cannot simply remain totally inarticulate, but must always seek to be expressed, if always inadequately, in the realm of the categorical. Or to put it differently, we must always try to express our transcendental experience. The expression can take place in language – in philosophy or poetry – or through other means – art, music, religious symbols and actions.[3] The attempt to articulate always in some way fails – the articulation can never be adequate to the original experience. But the attempt must nevertheless always be made. Furthermore, the attempt itself is important. The very expression of the experience, Rahner maintains, is always a shaping moment in the experience: what is experienced is partly determined by how this experience is expressed.

Something of an analogy can be found in the emotions. Having the experience of being in love (or of being angry) is not the same thing as describing the experience. An emotion is just fundamentally different from a concept. But the two things are not therefore unrelated. The experience of love will in fact be very much *shaped* by the way it is articulated, by the kind of expression it is given: it will make quite a difference to what someone experiences, for instance, depending on whether she names it a crush or a once-in-a-lifetime true love. And it may make quite a difference to the experience what culture the person lives in, and so what concepts of love or related emotions are in fact *available* to her. The emotion and the conceptualization, then, are different – the latter never completely captures the former – but the conceptualization has a *formative* effect on the emotion itself. The analogy is far from perfect, of course, because transcendental experience is not one thing among others in the way that, for instance, anger is one emotion among others.

In some ways a stronger analogy can be found in the notion of an all-pervasive *mood*. A mood colours and shapes the whole of one's experience, and yet precisely because it is so all-pervasive one can be almost unaware of it. A person can return to a city in which she once lived, for example, and, seeing the old familiar landmarks, suddenly realize for the first time that she had been unhappy when living there. At the time she may only have been aware of the particular goals she was working towards, the particular problems she was confronting, the ever-changing day-to-day concerns, and not of the underlying mood which was colouring *all* of these activities and the whole of her existence. But that does not make the mood unreal or unimportant: though unnoticed, it may have been far more important in shaping her experience than the more obvious daily goings on. In a similar way our transcendental experience is all-pervasive, all-important, and yet easily missed:

> what is most basic and original and most self-evident can also be what is most able to be overlooked and is most able to be suppressed. (FCF 29)

And just as it may be easier to concentrate on one's day-to-day activities than to ask if one is fundamentally happy, so we may not in fact particularly *want* to be aware of our transcendental experience. Life may be simpler if we ignore it:

[many people] live at a distance from themselves in that concrete part of their lives and of the world around them which can be manipulated and controlled. They have enough to do there, and it is very interesting and important. And if they ever reflect at all on anything which goes beyond all this, they can always say that it is more sensible not to break one's head over it. (FCF 32)

In one sense Rahner's basic picture of the human being, whether set out in terms of the *Vorgriff* or of our orientation to mystery or of our transcendental experience, is extraordinarily optimistic: everyone is at all times having to do with God, experiencing God, aware of God. Not just mystics, but all human beings have a profound and continuous connection to God. But in another way the picture is not quite so positive: if everyone is at all times having to do with God, experiencing God, aware of God, it is also true that no one ever has to do with God, experiences God, is aware of God in the way in which we have to do with, experience or are aware of anything or anyone else.

This is a point on which Rahner insists again and again, a point which all his images underline and which all his talk of mystery is intended to reinforce: God is never known in the way that objects are known. The infinity towards which the mind moves is never grasped in the same way as are the objects which become knowable in this movement. The light is never known directly, but only *in* its illumination of particular, concrete objects. The light is only known *as* that which lights up what we see before us. The ever-present mystery of our existence can never be penetrated and grasped; it can never be *solved*, so that it ceases to be a mystery. The horizon is never known itself as

11

an object, for every knowing of an object occurs against the background of the horizon. The horizon, as Rahner sometimes puts it, always recedes – if we try to grasp it, to talk about it, to think about it directly, we are necessarily using words and concepts which are really only appropriate for objects. If we try to grasp the horizon, if we try to speak of it or to focus our vision on it, we find that what we have in fact got is again an object, something that is itself only known against the horizon. The horizon of our knowing cannot itself become an object *within* the horizon. God, in short, is never known as one thing among others. God cannot ever be for us 'a member of the larger household of all reality'. Rahner suggests indeed that atheists are perfectly right in denying the existence of God if it is this sort of God, a God who can exist side by side with the things in the world, that they think they are denying.

 So there is a sense in which what Rahner gives with one hand he takes away with the other. In one sense we always have God, in another sense we never do. God is always present but never grasped, always there but never as something we can get into focus, always experienced but never pinned down.

Another way to get at the same point is to say that Rahner has an unusual understanding of the kind of thing that religious experience is. Ordinarily we think of religious experience as some sort of 'peak' experience, something that is strange and that bowls us over. We may think along the lines of Rudolf Otto's classic account of religious experience as an encounter with the 'numinous', with a *mysterium fascinans* and *tremendum*, something both fascinating and terrifying. Ordinarily, at the very least, we think of religious experience as something that lifts us right out of everyday humdrum affairs. On Rahner's account it is not like that. We may have, or some of us may have, such 'peak' experiences, but these are not what is of decisive importance. The religious experience that really matters is the one that is always available, always there as an element *in* our ordinary humdrum affairs. And this of course means that religious experience is not such a dramatic and exciting thing as we usually think it to be.

What sort of practical advice, one might ask, would come out of the sort of vision we have been examining? Clearly Rahner would not suggest that people need to cultivate strange and unusual new religious experiences in order to get in touch with God. But what then? Would he tell his readers that they are already in touch with God, whether they know it or not, and so they can quite happily ignore the whole business? Or that they should perhaps sit staring at a chair and concentrating very hard, in the hope of becoming aware of the transcendental dimension of their experience? Neither of these possibilities has the ring of profound or practical spiritual advice, and in fact Rahner takes neither route. He suggests that though in some sense the experience of God is always present, it is not always equally obvious to us. There are certain situations in which it comes to the fore, in which it is easier for us to become aware of it, and it is by paying attention to these that a person can deepen her religious life. Rahner mentions such things as boredom, loneliness, fear (especially all-encompassing fear), the imminence of death, the sense of absolute responsibility, and also, on a less negative note, the experience of 'surpassing joy' (TI XVII 236). These are things which must be faced and not suppressed and run away from, if we really want to make our own the experience of God. In these sorts of experiences, Rahner seems to suggest, we are brought face to face with the limitations of the things of this world, with the finiteness of all finite things, and so it is these that we can most clearly become conscious of our own transcendence of, our own 'going beyond', all that is limited and finite.

Rahner never offers a proof of the existence of God. But if he is right, no such proof is needed, for everyone (to put the point a little bluntly) already believes in God, whether they know it or not. All very well, one might say, but then this claim *itself* needs to be proved. Rahner needs to *convince* us of the fact that we all really do have this '*Vorgriff*', this all-pervasive awareness of God.

How he might try to convince us of this, of course, is something I have so far not spelled out. At the risk of making Rahner appear rather arbitrary I have avoided discussion of the philosophical arguments he offers to support his claims. There are several reasons for this. In spite of what one might think, they are not very important. Obviously, they would be extremely important if they were really persuasive. Anyone who could give a water-tight, knock-down argument showing that everyone really, on some level, believes in God would have done something very significant indeed. Anyone who could in this way prove that proofs of God's existence were unnecessary would revolutionize the worlds of philosophy and theology. But not many people are persuaded that Rahner has done this. Not many people, moreover, are interested in Rahner's thought because of these sorts of arguments. It is the picture he develops, and the *uses* to which he puts it, which are interesting. In fact this picture turns out to be a highly versatile tool, one which allows Rahner to approach a variety of issues in new and provocative ways. For instance, Rahner rethinks the whole concept of revelation by developing his distinction between the transcendental and the categorical realms of experience. Who Christ is, what grace is, what happens to non-Christians – all these questions, as we shall see in chapters to come, can be approached afresh with the help of this one idea. Rahner's conception of the human being is best judged, then, not by the questionable arguments he offers for it, or not mainly by these, but by its fruit in the whole of his thought.

2

Christ and grace

It is characteristic of Christianity to make claims of absolute uniqueness for Jesus Christ, and it is characteristic of modern people to feel uneasy about this. It would not be a problem, perhaps, to say that Jesus was one among many good people, one among many prophets, one among many heroes who have been willing to go even to the point of death for the sake of others. It would not be a problem to put Jesus on a list of the world's great saintly figures, to speak in one breath of Gautama Buddha, Socrates, Jesus, St Francis, Gandhi and Martin Luther King. It might not even be a problem to think of Jesus as an incarnation of God – provided it was precisely *an* incarnation, one among many, as some strands of Hinduism envisage. But to say of this one ancient Near-Eastern carpenter that he is *the* incarnation of God, the *only* one, that in him and him alone we can find our salvation, this is troublesome. The world shows a certain regularity, and we are inclined to meet with suspicion any claims to have found an absolute break in its regularity.

One way to understand Rahner's writings on Christ is to see them as efforts to deal with this problem. Rahner is sufficiently committed to traditional Christianity that there is for him no option but to speak of Christ with phrases beginning 'the absolute . . .', 'the unique . . .', 'the sole . . .', and so on. Simply throwing away the bits that cause us difficulties is not a possibility. But at the same time he is sufficiently concerned about what is and what is not credible to modern people to feel the need to confront the difficulties this creates. A certain pattern emerges in Rahner's writings, partly in response to these two commitments: while Christ is assumed to be absolutely unique, he must nevertheless be shown to be very much a part of the fabric of things. Christ is unique and yet not discontinuous with the rest, unique and yet integrated into a broader picture. In one case which we shall consider – Rahner's attempted solution to the classical problem of the two natures (divine and human) of Christ – what is most distinctive about Christ is understood within the context of a wider picture of what it is to be human. In another case – Rahner's treatment of Christ's role in our salvation – Christ is integrated into a broader vision of God's single, overarching movement towards the world in grace.

I have said that all this is *one* way to understand Rahner's writings on Christ, and the qualification is important. It is in fact not only Rahner's concerns for issues of credibility that drive his Christology. At least as important is the need to take seriously what Christians believe about Christ, and work out the radical and far-ranging implications of this. In other words, this pattern of integrating Christ *into* a broader picture can equally be described as a pattern of shaping a broader vision *around* what is found in Christ.

Fully human and fully divine

Rahner affirms, with the Christian tradition, the full divinity as well as the full humanity of Jesus Christ. Jesus, and he alone of all the people who have walked the earth, is divine. In this sense, he is what the rest of us are not – he stands alone, utterly different. And yet Rahner proposes a way of *interpreting* the divinity and the humanity of Jesus so that one can say, not only 'he is what the rest of us are not', but also, 'he is what the rest of us *are*, only more so'. We can think about Christ, Rahner wants to persuade us, in such a way that our understanding of who he is can be thoroughly integrated into our understanding of who we are.[1]

It is typical of Rahner that he nowhere tries to *prove* Christ's divinity, or even to argue that if one weighs up the probabilities it is more likely than not that he was divine. He simply takes as his starting point what has been accepted in most Christian churches since the Council of Chalcedon in 451, namely that Christ is 'truly God and truly man . . . two natures without confusion, without change, without division, without separation'. Rahner's question is then not 'Is this true?' but instead 'What does it mean?'

It has to be said that this second question is by no means an easy one. One might suppose that at the very least the people at the Council of Chalcedon who came up with this 'two natures' formulation knew what they meant by it, but this is not necessarily so. The Council of Chalcedon came at the end of a lengthy period of struggle between opposing theological factions, and its definition represented something more like a compromise formula which was just about acceptable to most of the parties involved, than a description of a definite vision of how the divine and the human meet in Jesus. Those on each side of the struggle may well have had reasonably well-worked-out visions, but they were different visions, and each side was highly suspicious of what was promoted by the other. The formula quoted above was acceptable, then, because it ruled out to the satisfaction of each what each considered to be the most heretical tendencies of the other, and not because it proposed a new vision of Jesus' divinity and humanity with which all sides could be happy. The Council of Chalcedon, one could say, decided upon a formula, and left it to the future to work out what that formula meant.

So how can this formula be understood? It has to be said again that this is no easy matter. Chalcedon seems to block off all the obvious routes to an explanation of how Jesus is both divine and human. One cannot, for instance, say that since Jesus had God as his father and Mary as his mother he was some sort of half-and-half mixture, divine in some respects and human in others. The Chalcedonian formula insists that he was wholly the one *and* wholly the other, not any kind of hybrid. Or again, what options are left to us if we are told that the two natures are *neither* confused (i.e. mixed) *nor* separated?

At this point most Christians might be content to acknowledge that there is a paradox at the heart of the gospel. That Jesus is both human and divine is simply a truth of faith to be believed but not comprehended. They do not understand it, but then they do not *expect* to understand it, and do not *need* to understand it.

There is a certain danger associated with such a complacent acceptance of paradox, however. It may be that one cannot help but have some picture of what is meant by saying that Jesus is both divine and human. Perhaps it is not possible to affirm a paradox and also keep one's mind entirely empty of any idea about what it means. After all, if a Christian talks about Jesus, meditates on the life of Jesus and prays to Jesus, he will inevitably be working from *some* sort of idea of who Jesus is. The danger is, then, that one does in fact have an understanding of what the Chalcedonian formula means – a picture of the way in which Jesus is human and divine – but because this understanding is not consciously acknowledged one cannot evaluate it or take responsibility for it.

As Rahner reads the situation, most ordinary Christians do indeed have some picture of how divine and human meet in Christ. Not only that, but this picture is heretical. Rahner suggests that most Christians today are closet *docetists.* Docetism was a tendency firmly rejected by the early Church to deny the full humanity of Jesus, to see Christ as only apparently human. Contemporary Christians may be verbally orthodox, Rahner suggests, and toe the Chalcedonian line, but in practice they think of Christ simply as God in human clothing, as God having dressed himself up in a human exterior in order to make himself visible to the world. And it is because of this misunderstanding, Rahner suggests, that many people find the

Church's teaching about Christ unworthy of belief. It takes on the ring of mythology: God had to come to earth in a human livery because there was a problem he could not solve from heaven.

The solution that Rahner tries to develop draws on the kinds of ideas described in the previous chapter. He thinks, in other words, that if one starts with the right sort of picture of the human being then the apparent paradox of the two natures of Christ can be resolved. What has to be rejected is the idea that human nature is something clearly defined and limited, something that one can set within boundaries and specify exactly. If this were human nature then the Chalcedonian problem would probably be insuperable, because it is not at all clear how God could become something thus circumscribed and delimited and yet still in any sense be God. But in fact human nature cannot be defined in this way – it is not thus closed in on itself:

> one can only say what man is by expressing what he is con-
> cerned with and what is concerned with him. But that is
> the boundless, the nameless. (TI IV 108)

Here, then, the ideas of the previous chapter begin to make their reappearance. It is in the nature of the human being to be a kind of infinite openness. Always in the encounter with the finite we are striving beyond it towards the infinite, always at our very centre we are directed towards that which lies beyond the world, towards God:

> When we have said everything about ourselves that can
> be described and defined, we have still said nothing about
> ourselves, unless we have included or implied the fact that
> we are beings who are referred to the incomprehensible
> God. (TI IV 108)

Now, if this is what it is to be human in general, if this is of the *essence* of being human, then the normally paradoxical Chalcedonian doctrine comes to seem not quite so difficult.

Christ can be seen, on Rahner's account, as the radicalization, the supreme case, of what is true of us all. If to be oriented towards God is what makes us human, then the one who is so oriented towards God that he is utterly given over to God, and utterly taken over by God, is actually the one who is at the same time the most fully human. So the divinity of Christ can be conceived not as the contradiction of Christ's humanity, but as its ultimate fulfilment. To be human is to transcend all things, to 'go beyond' all things towards God: when this transcendence, this 'going beyond', is carried to its single, highest and most radical instance, then in that case to be human simply is to be God: 'The incarnation of God is . . . the unique, *supreme*, case of the total actualization of human reality' (TI IV 110).

What Rahner wants to persuade us of, then, is that we can think of Christ, not as an incomprehensible oddity, and not as God in a human disguise, and not as simply a paradox, but as the extreme case of what it is to be human, as like us only more so, as what we are if you take it all the way to its limit. Christ's divinity, he wants to say, is something which on the one hand belongs only to Christ – something unique and absolute – but which on the other hand can be situated within the much broader phenomenon of the common humanity of us all.[2]

One might ask whether this actually works. Is the difference between Jesus and us just a matter of degree, and if so can it really make sense to talk about Christ as absolutely unique? And what stops the rest of us from also being God if this is a possibility built into human nature? We are in a rather murky territory here, and it is not clear whether Rahner's position is defensible, but before too quickly dismissing him it might be worth exploring a little further the way these slippery notions of 'difference of degree' and 'possibility built into human nature' work. Consider for instance the people – often so-called *idiots savants* – capable of extraordinary arithmetical feats, such as multiplying huge numbers almost instantaneously. They are human beings and not, presumably, employing magical means to solve problems, and so it must be said of them that they are fulfilling some possibility built into human nature. And it can also be said that the difference between them and the rest of us is 'only' one of degree: we can multiply one- or perhaps two-digit numbers almost instantaneously, they can manage twelve. And yet we are not on a continuum with them: there is for some reason a really drastic difference between them and us. It is quite possible, in other words, to talk about a difference of degree which is nevertheless a radical difference, and one can talk about the fulfilment of a possibility built into human nature without automatically suggesting that any of us could achieve this fulfilment if only we tried a little harder.[3]

Christ and grace

Just as Rahner believes that who Christ is can be integrated into a broader picture, so also, he thinks, can what Christ *does*, Christ's role in the history of salvation. In particular, Rahner places Christ within an overarching account of how God 'gives himself' to the world in grace. In Rahner's view grace is not to be seen as something which is first offered to humanity as a consequence of Christ's incarnation, death and resurrection. Instead the notion of grace is the broader context within which we can make sense of Christ's life and death. The incarnation is not as Rahner presents it the trigger for God's *becoming* gracious to us, but the peak of God's *being* gracious to us.[4]

To fill out this picture we need to begin by looking a little more closely at the notion of grace. In particular it is worth mentioning three features of Rahner's understanding of grace, or to be more precise, three features of Rahner's later understanding of grace. (Grace is one of those topics to which Rahner returns again and again, and about which he did not always say exactly the same thing.)

First of all, according to Rahner grace is, most fundamentally, God's 'self-communication'. What Rahner means by this can most easily be seen by way of contrast. Much of the time people use the word 'grace' in connection with some particular help or particular gift from God. With the help of God's grace, someone might say, I was able to give up this or that bad habit, this or that sin. One may hope that if a difficult situation arises one will be given the grace to know how to respond properly. One may hope that God will be gracious and forgive one's sins. Rahner would say that all these are legitimate ways to speak about grace, but that they all stem from something more basic and more profound. The most important thing that God gives in grace is not this or that particular gift, but God's very *self*, and Rahner describes this gift of himself as God's 'self-communication'.[5] From this one central gift flow the other more particular things which can also, in a secondary sense, be described by the word grace. A result of the fact that God gives himself to people and dwells in them, in other words, is that they are gradually transformed, so that they may over time overcome bad habits and particular sins, and so on.

With his insistence on the centrality of the notion of self-communication Rahner is wanting to reverse the way of thinking about grace which prevailed in the neo-scholastic theology in which he had himself been trained. Neo-scholastic theology operated with a distinction between one kind of grace, by which God alters and transforms us, and a second kind of grace, in which God actually 'bestows himself' upon us and 'dwells within' us. There were various ways of working out the precise relationship between the two categories of grace, but what all agreed upon was that the first kind of grace was the preparation for, and basis of, the second: God first changes us, and then enters into a new relationship of union with us – God's 'indwelling in the soul' follows as a *consequence* of the prior (at least logically prior) transformation of the soul. These two kinds of grace were described respectively as 'created' and 'uncreated' grace, and so the standard neo-scholastic view was that uncreated grace followed upon, and was in some sense a *reward for*, the transformation which created grace brought about in a person. The more biblical view, Rahner maintains, is that created grace flows from uncreated grace. The spirit of God dwells in us, and as a result, 'as a consequence and a manifestation' of this divine self-communication, we are transformed concretely and in particular ways. God transforms us by giving himself to us, rather than giving himself to us *because* he has transformed us.

This difference in ordering corresponds to an important difference in emphasis. The tendency of neo-scholastic theology was to see uncreated grace, God's communication of himself to the soul, as secondary and derivative, and so to concentrate its attention almost exclusively on created grace. To reverse the ordering is by contrast to place uncreated grace, God's self-communication, at the centre of the picture. What is new in Rahner's approach, then, is not the distinction between particular (created) gifts and God's giving of himself, but the *centrality* which Rahner gives to the latter. And he would say that even this is not in fact new, but a return to something closer to the outlook of St Paul and of the church Fathers.

A second distinctive feature of Rahner's understanding of grace has to do with where Rahner *locates* grace, with where he understands grace to be offered and perhaps received. God's self-communication to us occurs most fundamentally, Rahner thinks, on the level of our 'transcendental experience'. That is to say, in that region of our experience where we always go beyond all particular finite objects, on that level where we always have, whether we realize it or not, an awareness of God, there grace is offered and either accepted or rejected. Rahner is led to this position by two considerations: on the one hand he wants to say that grace is *experienced*, and on the other hand he believes that by its nature grace cannot be experienced as one experience among others.

First, then, it is important for Rahner to be able to insist that grace actually is *experienced*. Rahner was unhappy with the understanding prevalent in the Catholicism of the first half of the twentieth century, according to which grace occurred, one might say, behind the believer's back. Grace was something in which a good Catholic believed but which had nothing to do with anything she could be aware of. One might trust that in, say, going to mass one was receiving grace, but this was not something that could actually be *felt*. Having received grace would make a big difference when one died, but very little in the meantime. It too easily became, therefore, a very theoretical matter, something which in the day-to-day living of life made no impact whatsoever.

So grace must be able to be experienced – it must really affect us in the here and now. But on the other hand, if grace is actually God's giving of *himself*, it cannot be experienced as one thing among many others, as a particular experience we might have among, and on the same level as, all our other experiences, for God is not one object among others, a 'member of the larger household of all reality'. So grace must enter into our experience, but it cannot do so as one experience on a par with others. The only alternative, then, is that it must be experienced on the transcendental level, never directly but always in all our other experiences, always in the background, always part of the general texture of our experience rather than the outstanding features of it.

How, then, does this work? How exactly can grace be experienced on a transcendental level? As we saw in Chapter 1, on Rahner's account it is part of our basic structure always to be related to God in all our dealings with the things of the world. This basic structure cannot itself be described as grace, for this is built into our very nature as human beings, and grace must be a gift, something which is not owed to us, something which goes *beyond* our basic nature. So Rahner describes grace as a 'modification of our transcendence': even without grace we would have been aware of God, but not in the same way. God's self-communication to us has the effect of altering our relationship to our horizon, to the 'mystery' which surrounds us. *How* precisely is it altered? Here Rahner becomes elusive, and his language rather slippery: God becomes for us, he says, not just the infinitely distant goal of all our striving, but the goal which 'draws near' and 'gives itself'. Whatever these phrases might mean, they do *not*, Rahner insists, mean that God becomes another object in the world which we can control. The God who gives himself in grace remains a mystery: grace is

> the grace of the *nearness* of the abiding mystery: it makes God accessible in the form of the holy mystery and presents him thus as the incomprehensible. (TI IV 56)

Without ceasing to be God, in other words, and therefore ungraspable and incomprehensible, God somehow draws near and offers himself to us.

Grace, then, is to be understood as God's self-communication to us, and it is to be understood as occurring at the level of our transcendental experience. The third important feature of Rahner's account of grace is its *universality*. According to Rahner, grace is not offered to some of us some of the time, but to all of us all of the time. The alteration in our relationship to our horizon, the drawing near of the goal of all our striving, this is not something that sometimes happens and sometimes does not, so that on good days God draws near and on others remains aloof. And it is not something which is given to some and withheld from others. It is a constant feature of all human beings' experience, though it is a feature which can be resisted:

> grace . . . always surrounds man, even the sinner and the unbeliever, as the inescapable setting of his existence. (TI IV 181)

The distinction, then, between what we are like by nature and what we are like by grace is only a theoretical one, for one never finds a human being in a state of pure nature. Our experience is always already, on Rahner's account, affected by grace. We have a tendency to assume that to be special grace must somehow also be limited, but Rahner thinks there is no really good reason for this assumption:

> ... it is quite conceivable that the whole spiritual life of man is constantly affected by grace. It is not a rare and sporadic event just because grace is unmerited. Theology has been too long and too often bedevilled by the unavowed supposition that grace would be no longer grace if it were too generously distributed by the love of God! (TI IV 180)

Grace, then, always surrounds us and always affects us. But this is not to say that we all stand in exactly the same situation with regard to grace, for there remains the question of the response we make to the offer of grace. We have a fundamental freedom either to accept God's self-communication or to reject it. If we reject it, however, we do not make it go away, but instead live in permanent contradiction with it. We are all always surrounded by grace, then, but we may not all be equally in what is traditionally called a 'state of grace'.

Our response to grace, our acceptance or rejection of it, is something that goes on at a very deep level. It is not one deliberate decision we make among others, but our most fundamental decision which shapes all that we do. And it is a decision that we may be unaware of, and that we may make without even having heard of the concept of grace.

So far I have been describing grace in terms of God's self-communication to *individuals*, but it can also be described as God's self-communication to the world as a whole. We can imagine God as taking millions upon millions of separate decisions to bestow grace on individuals, but we can also think of a single decision to communicate himself to the world which is worked out through the human race as a whole and each individual separately. And if we think of grace as the result of God's one decision to communicate himself, then we begin to be in a position to see how Christ comes into the picture. God's single movement towards the world reaches its *peak*, Rahner says, in Jesus Christ. In his incarnation the self-communication which is always on offer to all people at all times reaches its high point.

Why does it need to have a high point? In Christ, Rahner maintains, God's self-communication becomes definitive, and it becomes irreversible. If we were to look only to our own experience of grace, we could never be absolutely sure – we could never be sure that we had really accepted the offer, or that God had really completely committed himself. God could always remain free to change his mind, to repent of his graciousness. Rahner sometimes speaks of an 'ongoing dialogue' with freedom on both sides. With Christ the dialogue has not reached an end, but it has reached a point where there is no going back. In him 'the success, the victory and the irreversibility of this process [of God's self-communication] has become manifest in and in spite of this ongoing dialogue of freedom' (FCF 194). In Christ we see God absolutely committing himself to us, and in Christ we also see a human being, one of us, definitively and absolutely *accepting* God's self-gift.

Rahner is not trying to suggest that God remains uncertain about whether he will carry through with his self-communication until he sees what Christ does. The idea is rather that *because* God means to carry through, to communicate himself fully to the world, his self-communication reaches a point of absolute commitment in Christ. Jesus does not change God's mind. Jesus does not turn God's wrath to mercy. Christ's death does not *persuade* God to be gracious, but is itself an expression, or rather *the* definitive expression, of God's graciousness. The incarnation is a high point in the history of salvation rather than a turning point.

An interesting question is whether on this account one can speak of Christ as in any way the *cause* of God's graciousness to us and therefore of our salvation. To be unable to do so would be to find oneself in a rather awkward position as a Christian theologian. Rahner's answer would be that it depends on what precisely one means by the word 'cause'. Christ is not the trigger for our salvation. He is not what first *persuades* God to be gracious to us. And so in the most ordinary sense of the word he is not its cause. On the other hand, if Christ is the peak, the high point, even the *goal* of God's self-communication to the world, it is possible to speak of this whole self-communication as *aiming* at Christ, as occurring for the sake of the incarnation. In so far as Christ is the goal of the one divine movement that brings about our salvation, then he can indeed be thought of as the cause of this salvation. Christ is, in technical (Aristotelian) terms, not the 'efficient' but the 'final cause' of our salvation.

Rahner in fact carries this idea one step – one large step – further. It is possible to think of creation itself, of the whole world and all that is in it, as existing for the sake of Christ. God wills, or so the story goes, to communicate himself to that which is not God, and this self-communication to the other is achieved definitively in the incarnation, when in a particular human being God and the world become one, without ceasing to be what they each are. But in order to communicate himself to that which is not-God, God first has to bring this not-God, i.e. the world, into existence. So God does not first create the world and then, as a kind of after-thought, in response to what goes on in the world, decide to become incarnate. Instead God from the beginning creates what is other than himself in order to give himself to it. This is all highly speculative, of course, and Rahner does not pretend to offer any definitive arguments. He simply suggests that it is a possible approach:

> we are perfectly entitled to think of the creation and of the incarnation, not as two disparate, adjacent acts of God . . . but as two moments and phases in the real world of the unique, even though internally differentiated,

process of God's self-renunciation and self-expression into what is other than himself. (TI V 177–8)

We began this chapter with the notion that Rahner's inclination is to integrate Christ into a broader picture. With the suggestion that the whole world was created for the sake of the incarnation that tendency is taken to its extreme, but it is also in a certain sense reversed – now it is everything else that is to be integrated into our understanding of Christ.

There is an interesting point of convergence here between Rahner and the greatest of twentieth-century Protestant thinkers, Karl Barth. For the most part the two theologians seem to go in opposite directions. While Rahner locates an experience of God at the very heart of our human nature, and thinks it vitally important to link theology to this experience, Barth vehemently rejects modern anthropocentrism: 'one can *not*', insists Barth, 'speak of God simply by speaking of man in a loud voice'.[6] Yet in suggesting that the world itself was brought into being for the sake of the incarnation, Rahner is proposing very much what Barth does with his notion that 'creation is for the sake of the covenant'.

An interesting feature of Rahner's approach to the incarnation is the role that sin plays – or rather the role that sin does not play – in the story. God's becoming incarnate in the world is not first and foremost a response to the problem posed by sin. It is instead a climactic moment in a *positive* movement towards the world, a movement which would have taken place even had there been no such thing as sin. Had Adam not fallen, to put it in traditional language, Christ would still have come into the world, would still have died, and would still have risen again. Rahner does not deny the reality or the gravity of sin and evil, nor does he deny that, in fact, the incarnation, cross and resurrection have something to do with the forgiveness of sin. But this is not all that they are; Christ is not *just* the remedy for our sins. Sin, as Rahner sees it, cannot be allowed to be the driving motor of the story of God's involvement with the world.

3

The Church and the world

What are the boundaries of the Church? Who is in and who is out? In the fifth century St Augustine introduced a distinction, which has been taken up repeatedly over the ages, between the visible and the invisible Church. The visible Church is the Church of all those who profess Christianity and are baptized – it is the Church as we can see it, the institutional church, the church as we must deal with it. The invisible Church, known only to God, is the community of the elect – the *true* Christians, those who will in fact be saved on the last day. The assumption has been that the invisible Church is a subset of the visible; the elect are some portion, a portion known to God and to no one else, of those who profess Christianity. Rahner reverses this idea. There is something like an invisible Church as well as a visible, on his account, but the invisible is *broader* than the visible. The invisible Church is not the hidden kernel existing within the visible, but an extension of the Church beyond the boundaries of those who explicitly confess Christianity.

The starting point for Rahner's reflections is a problem which confronts most thoughtful contemporary Christians. On the one hand Christianity emphatically insists that there is no salvation apart from Christ and apart from faith, no salvation outside the Church. On the other hand the Christian is aware both of individuals and of whole societies who, through no fault of their own, have not embraced Christian teachings, and finds it impossible to imagine a good and loving God simply consigning them to perdition. We are told in Scripture that God wills the salvation of all human beings (1 Timothy 2.4). How are we to reconcile this with the traditional claim that there is no salvation outside the Church?

The difficulty has not always been felt with equal force. For many centuries it was simply a given, an unquestioned assumption, that God's justice required the damnation of the mass of fallen humanity – but this no longer strikes us as so obvious. And in recent times we have become much more acutely aware of entire cultures and peoples for whom Christianity has not been, and perhaps still is not, a genuinely live option.

One approach might be to suppose that while faith in Christ is necessary for salvation in principle, God in his mercy makes an exception for those who have not heard of Christ, or who have not had a meaningful encounter with Christianity. Rahner however rejects any such easy solution:

> The Christian is convinced . . . that this faith [in Christ] is not merely a positive commandment from which one could be dispensed under certain conditions; that membership in the one true Church does not constitute a merely extrinsic condition from which it would be appropriate for someone to be freed by the mere fact that he does not and cannot know about it and its necessity. (TI IV 390)

The problem with such an approach is that it presents faith in Christ as not *really*, not *ultimately*, necessary for salvation, but just a condition which God happens to impose and so can dispense with at will. Rahner insists that this is not how faith must be understood:

> faith is in itself necessary and therefore demanded absolutely, not merely as a commandment but as the only possible means, not as a condition alone but as an unavoidable way of access, for man's salvation is nothing less than the fulfilment and definitive coming to maturity of

precisely this beginning, for which therefore nothing else can substitute. (TI VI 391)

Faith in Christ is *intrinsically* related to salvation: it is built into the very nature of the thing that salvation must be linked to faith. It makes no sense, then, to suppose that God might dispense with this particular requirement in some cases. A parent might from time to time make an exception to the rule that those who do not eat their dinner do not get any dessert, but there can be no exception to the principle that those who do not learn the alphabet will not learn to read, and Rahner is suggesting that the link between faith and salvation is more like the latter than the former.

If one cannot get away from the need for faith in Christ and membership of the Church, however, one can think again about what faith and church membership actually mean. There must be degrees of church membership, Rahner suggests,

> not only in ascending order from being baptized, through the acceptance of the fullness of the Christian faith . . . but also in descending order from the explicitness of baptism into a non-official and anonymous Christianity which can and should yet be called Christianity in a meaningful sense, even though it itself cannot and would not describe itself as such. (TI VI 391)

If church membership is necessary for salvation then, reasons Rahner, it must be a possibility for all people, and if an explicit church membership is not a real possibility for some people then there simply must be some other kind of church membership. Similarly, if faith in Christ is necessary for salvation but explicit, professed faith is not a real possibility for all, then there simply must be something which is *not* explicit and professed faith and yet which still is faith in Christ.

So what exactly could this implicit faith in Christ be? What does 'anonymous Christianity' look like? Rahner's understanding of how an implicit membership of the Church and an implicit faith are possible is based very much on the sorts of ideas we have already been considering in the previous two chapters. We saw in Chapter 1 that Rahner believes all human beings to have some sort of awareness of God, and that this awareness is not like our awareness of other things, but something that is so all-pervasive that it is elusive and easily missed. So on Rahner's understanding it is possible to have such an awareness and yet on the level of explicit, professed belief to be an agnostic or even an atheist. Now, taken on its own such an awareness of God is not enough to make anyone an anonymous Christian. At best it can make someone – even an agnostic or an atheist – an 'anonymous theist'. What is important is that we not only have an implicit awareness of God, but also an implicit experience of *grace*. As we saw in Chapter 2, Rahner understands grace to be God's drawing near to us and communicating himself to us, and he understands this communication to take place in our 'transcendental experience', in that region of our experience where we have to do not with particular objects but with God. Now this grace must be considered to be the grace of Christ, Rahner maintains, since it is part of God's single movement towards the world which reaches its peak in Christ. So the grace of Christ is offered to all human beings in their transcendental experience.

This is still not quite enough to make all people anonymous Christians, and indeed Rahner holds back from making the claim that in fact all people are. There remains the question of what *response* is made to God's offer of grace – there remains the question of whether the grace is accepted (in what can be called faith) or refused. Now in order to respond to grace one does not first have to realize that there is such a thing as grace (or even that there is such a thing as God). The response, like the awareness of God and the awareness of grace, can once again be implicit. Because God's grace affects us at the very core of our being, Rahner maintains, we accept it if we fundamentally accept *ourselves*. So a person may think of herself as an atheist or a

Buddhist or a Parsi, but if in the depths of her being she accepts herself, then on Rahner's account she is an anonymous Christian.

One must be careful not to be misled by the term 'accepting oneself'. Though Rahner never offers a precise philosophical account of what he means by the phrase, it is quite clear that in his understanding it has less to do with self-acceptance in the sense that contemporary popular psychology is interested in it, than with the acceptance of pain and suffering and the acceptance of one's responsibilities and one's limitations.

Rahner's theory of anonymous Christianity has met with a great deal of interest, and with a great deal of criticism. It provides an unusual and creative solution to a problem which most thoughtful Christians confront, and it is a solution which has much to be said for it. In particular it allows one to avoid going down either of two more obvious routes, both of which can seem unattractive. One route is simply to accept the traditional teaching – outside the Church there is no salvation – and take a very grim view of the chances of the mass of humanity. The other is to abandon Christianity's traditional insistence on the centrality and uniqueness of Christ, and see all religions as equally good roads to God and to salvation. To those whose sense is that the first route is unloving and the second unfaithful, Rahner's suggestion can come as a welcome relief.

Many, however, do not find Rahner's proposal quite so pleasing. The theory of anonymous Christianity is often accused of condescension and of arrogance. The Christian who follows Rahner supposes he knows better than everyone else what they really believe and experience. He pays no attention to the differences of the different religions, but immediately claims them all as 'anonymous' versions of his own. The Christian can regard the Buddhist or the Hindu or the Jew as ultimately in the clear, ultimately saved, only because he regards these others as ultimately, however much they may protest to the contrary, believing what he believes.

These objections are at least partly based on misunderstanding. Critics tend not to view Rahner's notion of anonymous Christianity within the broader context of his theology, and they often take it to be an answer to quite a different question from the one Rahner asked. Where the critics concern themselves with the proper approach to inter-religious dialogue, Rahner was trying to deal with an intellectual, one could even say a pastoral, problem that arises *within* and *for* the Christian community. The issue he was grappling with was not, How should I talk to or argue with the Muslim and the Hindu?, but instead, How can I go on believing in God's goodness if I fear that the Muslim and Hindu are damned? (One of the earliest essays in which Rahner approached the notion of anonymous Christianity, in fact, had nothing whatsoever to do with questions about our attitudes towards different religions. It was entitled 'The Christian Among Unbelieving Relations', and took up the pastoral question of how to deal with the anxiety caused to a parent, for instance, when their child leaves the Church.)

The very term 'anonymous Christianity' has also caused a good deal of unnecessary difficulty. Rahner uses 'anonymous' as a quasi-technical philosophical term, in the sense in which it is used in the philosophy of Edmund Husserl, but in ordinary language it has rather different overtones. Rahner intended the word to indicate something of which one is not aware on an articulate level; ordinarily it suggests something which one does not *admit*. The anonymous author does not publicly acknowledge her authorship, but she herself *knows* she is the author. If Rahner's theory is understood as in any way analogous to this – the Hindu secretly knows she is a Christian, but will not own up – it becomes clearly offensive. But this is very far from what Rahner intends.

In part, Rahner's theory has been criticized because it has been misunderstood, then. But this is not the whole story. It cannot be denied that there is a touch of the arrogant and offensive in what Rahner maintains. No one, perhaps, can retain the traditional claims of the uniqueness and universal relevance of Christ without being vulnerable at some level to such charges. But by translating the traditional claim about the universal relevance of Christ into a claim about a universal pattern of *experience*, Rahner intensifies the problem.

Christians have always believed that all people, whether they know it or not, are created; that all people, whether they know it or not, are sinners; that all people, whether they know it or not, stand in need of redemption in Christ. This is bad enough. But to say that all people, whether they know it or not, whether they admit it or deny it, have certain kinds of *experience*, this is to take things a step further. Experience, we tend to think, is the one thing about which no one can dictate to others – it is the one thing about which each person is their own authority. And therefore it is bound to seem particularly problematic when someone comes along and makes claims, not only about his own experience or the experience of his own religious community, but about the experience of all people, whatever they themselves tell of their experience. Rahner is, admittedly, interested in a level of experience somewhat different from the one about which we usually think, but this does not entirely take away the difficulties his position causes.

One question which is put to Rahner's theory, then, is whether it can do justice to the otherness of other religions. Another question is whether it can do justice to Christianity itself. Does Christianity in the ordinary sense of the word – explicit Christian belief and practice, the visible Church – cease to have any importance if salvation is possible through a merely implicit Christianity? Could not everyone settle for being anonymous Christians and forget all the bother of thinking about Jesus and going to church on Sunday?

Rahner insists that the answer to these questions is 'no'. Anonymous Christianity, he maintains, always in some sense *wants* to become explicit Christianity. It may not be able to do so. It may be prevented by external circumstances. The anonymous Christian may not have heard of Christianity, or may not have heard in the right way. But an explicit faith is nevertheless the direction in which the anonymous faith wants to go. A visible, articulated Christianity is the fulfilment of anonymous Christianity, the higher stage towards which it moves. And when explicit Christianity is a real possibility, it must be accepted. One could not go on being an anonymous Christian while having explicitly rejected Christianity – if what one rejected really was Christianity, that is to say, and not some misunderstanding of it. The notion that there is such a thing as anonymous Christianity, then, can never become an excuse for a believer. It can in principle only provide a way of thinking about other people, and never a way of thinking about oneself.

4

Sacraments and symbols

There are seven sacraments, instituted by Christ. Or so the Roman
Catholic Church has taught since the Councils of Florence (1439)
and Trent (1545–63). And these sacraments are the means of
God's grace, the instruments through which grace is conferred
on the individual.

This is a rather awkward area of Catholic theology. Why seven
sacraments exactly, it might be asked, why not eight or six?
And where is the evidence that Christ himself instituted these
seven? How plausible is it to suppose that Jesus had anything
to do with, say, confirmation? Or if Christ did institute precisely
seven sacraments, why did it take so many centuries before
the Church realized this? Furthermore, is there not something
very disturbing about pinning down God's grace, tying it to the
performance of particular ceremonies and rites?

Rahner writes a great deal about the sacraments, and his
treatment of them is interesting for many reasons. One of
these, paradoxically, is that it is at times hard to understand
how this Rahner writing about the sacraments can also be the
Rahner who develops an absolutely universal understanding
of grace. Something of the 'unsystematic' nature of Rahner's
approach comes through here. It is not that he actually con-
tradicts himself, for in the end the different pieces can more
or less be fitted together. But it is not always clear along the way
how this will work. One reason for this is that Rahner does not
begin from his own system, asking how a notion of sacraments
can be fitted into it; he takes as his starting point instead the

understanding of the sacraments which is common in the Catholic Church, and the sorts of difficulties mentioned above, difficulties facing Catholic theology in general. This means that it can take a certain amount of work to see how the different parts of Rahner's thought fit together. But it also means that there is a breadth and freshness to Rahner's writings which would be lacking in those of someone who was interested only in his own system.

Another reason why Rahner's treatment of the sacraments is interesting is that it illustrates the way in which it is possible to be simultaneously a conservative and a radical thinker. In so far as he is a committed Catholic theologian for whom certain points are fixed, Rahner is a conservative. He accepts, for instance, that baptism, confirmation, the eucharist, ordination, marriage, confession and the anointing of the sick are sacraments, and only these – the Councils of Florence and Trent cannot be repealed. And he takes it as given that the sacraments work, as the Church teaches, *ex opere operato*, that is, independently of the merit, the 'goodness', of the people who administer them and the people who receive them. But Rahner is well aware of the difficulties these sorts of views raise. What makes him a radical is that in trying to cope with these difficulties he is willing to rearrange radically many of his audience's ordinary ways of thinking. So the fixed points of Catholicism remain fixed, but the overall vision which emerges from Rahner's theology can be anything but familiar.

One of the most obvious questions to ask about sacraments is the following: are the sacraments supposed to bring about something new, or do they merely remind the believer of what is already the case? Are they to be understood as causing grace, or merely as symbolizing it? Does baptism, for instance, change a person's status in God's eyes, or does it simply express their (or their parents') faith, and God's forgiving acceptance? Neither option seems particularly satisfactory. To say that sacraments *cause* grace is to introduce, it would seem, a rather magical and mechanical element into the relationship with God: the human being performs a certain rite and God automatically doles out the gifts. But if one insists that the sacraments merely express and remind the believer of a state of affairs which is already in existence, one seems to rob them of any real and deep significance.

Rahner's position is that this question itself is based on a false dichotomy. The sacraments, he maintains, in fact cause grace *by* symbolizing it. Now there is nothing new in saying that the sacraments both cause grace and symbolize it: this in fact is the standard Catholic teaching. What is important about Rahner's approach is his insistence that the two should not be thought of separately. It is not just that the sacraments symbolize grace and also cause it. Rather they cause grace precisely *in* symbolizing it.

One of the things at issue here is a general understanding of the nature of symbols. We tend to think of a symbol as separate from what it symbolizes: the thing is there, complete in itself, and the symbol comes along and simply signals that it is there. Rahner maintains that 'real symbols' do not work this way, but are intimately connected with what they symbolize.

Consider, by way of example, the kiss of lovers. The kiss symbolizes the love. But it is not just a signal of the existence of something completely distinct from itself – or if it is, one would have to describe it as not a very successful or meaningful kiss. A kiss makes real, makes concrete, the love which it expresses. The kiss, the symbol, is not external to the love which it symbolizes, but is part of it. Or consider the act of kneeling in prayer. It would be an over-simplification to suppose that the kneeling was merely an outer sign of an inner attitude. If this were the case, why would anyone bother? God, it is presumed, knows the inner attitude anyway. People kneel because, to some extent at least, kneeling brings about and makes real the attitude it expresses. In symbolizing contrition, or submission, or reverence, the kneeling in fact goes some way towards making the one who prays contrite, or submissive, or reverent.

In general, Rahner maintains, symbols should be thought of as making actual, real and present that which they symbolize. He acknowledges that not everything we normally call a symbol fits this pattern: there are some cases where there is no deep connection between the symbol and what is symbolized, some cases where the one is merely an arbitrary sign indicating the other. A flag symbolizes a country, or the start of a race. The dots and dashes of Morse code are symbols representing letters and words. But these, in Rahner's view, should be regarded as the exception, as secondary, less important, deficient kinds of symbols – or as he sometimes puts it, as signs rather than symbols. Proper, 'real' symbols not only indicate to the outside world that something exists, but make it present to itself. If I express myself, for example, I may be merely indicating to other people something about the state of my thoughts and emotions. But more often than not it is in expressing myself that I actually become aware, or more fully aware, of myself and of what I am feeling. In some sense I *need* to express myself, to externalize my experience in symbols, in order to become real to myself.

There are a number of objections one might make here. First of all, in some cases what we ordinarily call symbols are intimately bound up with what they symbolize, in others not. On what basis can it be said that the one kind are 'real' symbols and the others something secondary and deficient? Is this not a bit arbitrary and high-handed? One might respond that it does not actually matter: what is significant is that Rahner is making a distinction between two kinds of symbols, and by describing the one kind as real symbols and the other as symbols only in a secondary sense, he is simply indicating which kind he finds interesting.

But this does not really settle the matter. Rahner in fact makes extremely strong claims for his notion of symbols. It is not just that, as it happens, we sometimes see a pattern where the symbol makes present and concrete what it symbolizes. Rahner (who is nothing if not a bold thinker) maintains that deep down *everything* works like this. Everything expresses itself in order to become itself: 'all beings are by their nature symbolic' (TI IV 224).

A claim of this breadth is hard to evaluate. According to Rahner it is rooted in a way of thinking about the nature of being that comes from Thomas Aquinas, but it is clear that it also owes something to the thought of the nineteenth-century speculative philosopher Hegel, and one's reaction to Rahner's theory of the symbol will in part depend on how much sympathy one has for this whole way of thought. To a certain kind of mind it will all seem irritatingly vague and ambiguous; to another it may seem to capture something profound about the nature of things. One thing which may be a cause for unease is that the concrete examples of things which make present or real what they symbolize, the examples which do most to give some sense and meaning to this idea of the 'real symbol', are all drawn from the human sphere. Our emotions and feelings, and perhaps even we ourselves, sometimes become more real to us as we express ourselves. But to say that not just human beings but beings in general become real to themselves by expressing themselves in symbols is to make an extraordinary leap. Rahner, one might want to say, is guilty of anthropomorphizing on a breathtaking scale. Whether this is a fair complaint, however, is difficult to decide without first resolving deep questions about how one should even go about the business of thinking about 'being'.

In any case, whatever the philosophical merit of Rahner's theory of the symbol, it is not only or even mainly as a philosophical theory that he proposes it. Primarily he presents it as something which is of great use in a wide range of theological areas. Take for example the doctrine of the Trinity. The traditional understanding of the relation of the first and second persons of the Trinity – of the Father to the Son – can be translated, Rahner thinks, quite simply into the statement that the Son is the real symbol of the Father. Just as a symbol is neither identical with nor simply different from that which it symbolizes, so the Son is distinct from and yet one with the Father. Just as a symbol expresses what it symbolizes, so the Son, also called the 'Word' (or, to use the Greek term, 'the Logos'), can be called the self-expression of the Father. And just as a being becomes itself in being expressed in its symbol, so the Father would not be the Father without the Son.

The incarnation too can and should be understood in symbolic terms. In the incarnation God expresses or 'exteriorizes' himself in a human nature. There can be a tendency, Rahner suggests, to think of the humanity of Christ as a mere instrument of God, a tool which the second person of the Trinity takes up in order to convey a message to the world. In fact, however, Christ's humanity is not just a sign arbitrarily chosen to indicate the presence of God, but a real symbol of God. And it is because of this that Jesus himself (and not just what Jesus says or does) can genuinely be the revelation of God – because the humanity is a symbol of the divinity Christians can say that in Christ they do not just find some pointer to God, but actually encounter God himself. To say that the humanity of Christ is a symbol of God, Rahner suggests at one point, is simply to offer a commentary on the biblical text, 'He that sees me, sees the Father' (John 14.9; TI IV 237).

This is quite a powerful idea, but it must be said that Rahner is using his own notion of symbol a little bit loosely here.[1] In the context of the incarnation he cannot in fact allow the word to mean quite what it means elsewhere. In general, as we have seen, a symbol is supposed to make real and present that which it symbolizes. Furthermore, what is symbolized is made real and present to itself as well as to others. In general, then, beings *need* their symbols: in order to actualize themselves, to become fully what they are, they must express themselves. Love, to return to our earlier example, needs concrete expressions such as the kiss in order to 'realize' itself. Calling the humanity of Christ the symbol of God, therefore, might seem to imply that God needs to take on this humanity, that the second person of the Trinity only becomes fully real *in* this humanity. But this Rahner cannot say. He is committed to the traditional notion that God is complete in himself, sufficient unto himself, and not in any way dependent for his well-being on the world. The incarnation is something that God freely chooses to do, but it cannot be something that God *needs* to do – it cannot be a necessary element in God's self-realization. Christ's humanity is a symbol of God, then, only in a slightly weakened sense of the word.

It is worth mentioning that by beginning from what was outlined in the previous chapter, one can in fact find another way of speaking of the incarnation as a symbol. In the previous chapter we saw that Rahner presents Christ as the high point and the definitive expression of God's grace to the world, and in this sense also Christ can be thought of as a symbol, as the real symbol of grace.

One could go on multiplying examples. The sacraments, with which we began, are symbols. The Church, to which we shall return, is itself a symbol. In general human beings have a symbolic structure built into them:

> the bodily reality of man, and so his acts in the dimensions of space and time, history and society, [should be] conceived of as symbolic realities embodying his person and its primordial decisions. (TI IV 242–3)

To put the point in more old-fashioned language, our bodies are the real symbols of our souls.

Within the context of Rahner's sweeping theory of the symbol, then, the idea that the sacraments are symbols of grace, and that as symbols they make grace real and present and so in some sense 'cause' it, no longer seems particularly odd or problematic. Grace, like so much else, needs to be symbolized, to be made concrete and tangible, in order fully to be what it is. But this does not mean that all the problems surrounding the theory of the sacraments are done away with. One is still left with the question of what is so special about these particular sacraments. Why pick out these seven and no others? And how can one claim that Christ instituted them? To say that many (or all) things must become concrete in symbols, and that grace is among them, is not in itself to make sense of the very specific claims of Catholicism. Here we need to look at a second important feature of Rahner's understanding of the sacraments, namely his conception of their relationship to the Church.

All Roman Catholic thinkers will make some connection between the sacraments and the Church, of course, but they can do so in very different ways. One view (what Rahner describes as the 'average' view) is that the Church is connected to the sacraments simply because it is the institution with the authority to dispense them. The Church is where you go to get the sacraments. Rahner thinks that this understanding is too superficial, that there is in fact a more intrinsic and profound relationship. The Church itself, he suggests, *is* a sacrament. It is the primary, fundamental sacrament, and the particular sacraments – the sacraments in the usual sense of the word – can be thought of as flowing from, and deriving their meaning from, this basic character of the Church.

But what can it mean to say that the Church is a sacrament? What content does the notion of 'sacrament' retain if it is going to be used so broadly? The traditional formula is that the sacraments both signify and effect grace, which is to say, in Rahner's terminology, that they are real symbols of grace. Rahner is simply suggesting by extension that *anything* which is a real symbol of grace can in some sense be called a sacrament. The Church fits this description, he maintains, because of its connection to Christ. In Christ God's grace becomes definitively concrete and tangible in the world: in Christ it is possible, Rahner says,

> to point to a visible, historically manifest fact, located in space and time, and say . . . There the grace of God appears in our world of time and space. (CS 15)

The role of the Church, on Rahner's account, is to continue over time and in a social form this function of making grace tangible, of symbolizing grace. This is what it means to call the Church 'the body of Christ'. The grace which enters history in a definite way and becomes incarnate in Christ in turn needs to be made concrete in a socially organized community, for human beings are essentially social creatures.

Whatever one makes of this claim – and some will no doubt be inclined to think that by linking the Church so intimately with Christ Rahner takes a rather overblown view of its importance – it has the advantage of smoothing the way for an account of the sacraments in the ordinary sense of the word. The seven sacraments, Rahner suggests, are particular acts in which the primary sacrament, the Church, concretely expresses itself. When the Church does what is its business to do, namely to make grace concrete and present, and when it does this as fully and as formally as possible, then there occurs a sacrament in the usual sense of the word.

If one takes this view one does not have to argue that Christ instituted each of the sacraments individually and explicitly. Instead one only needs to accept that Christ intended to bring about the existence of the Church in general (a point which some might of course still want to debate) and therefore intended whatever follows from the nature of the Church. Furthermore, it is not necessary to argue in the abstract, starting only from a definition of the Church, that there had to be these seven and only these seven sacraments. That the sacraments are the most fundamental expression of what it is, Rahner maintains, is something that the Church has discovered about itself over time. Just as a person does not first work out who she is in the abstract and then act it out, but learns who she is as she lives her life from day to day, so the Church has come to a knowledge of itself over the course of its history. So the task of the theologian is not to find a deductive proof that precisely these seven sacraments are built into the nature of the

Church, but only to show that it is plausible to understand them, once they have in fact emerged, as fundamental expressions of the Church.

Earlier in the chapter I suggested that in the end the different pieces of Rahner's thought fit together quite neatly, and it is time now to investigate this. How can Rahner reconcile the 'specialness' of the seven sacraments with his belief that salvation is a real possibility for all people, whether or not they have come into contact with the Church and the sacraments? And how can he speak of the sacraments as the 'cause' of grace if he thinks that grace is in any case always and everywhere available in the depths of people's consciousness, in their 'transcendental experience'?

The answer, to put it very briefly, is that Rahner presents the sacraments as a special case of a much broader pattern. The grace which is experienced in the depths of our being must always somehow be made concrete: it must always be symbolized in something external. The experience of grace must in one way or another be expressed, and it only fully becomes what it is in being expressed. To use the language I introduced in Chapter 1, the grace experienced on the 'transcendental' level needs to find expression in 'categorical experience'.

Almost any kind of explicit religious act, then, actually has a 'sacramental' character. When a person prays, according to Rahner, she is not doing something entirely new and different from what she ordinarily does, but is rather trying to bring to expression the relatedness to God which is already a part of all her ordinary doings in the world. The prayer is a 'sacrament' of the relationship with God occurring in the depths of her being. Religious acts bring into focus and give a concreteness to the religious dimension which is always present in our experience.

Since Rahner does not believe that grace occurs only in those who are explicitly religious, he has to say that the experience of grace can come to expression also in non-religious ways, for instance in poetry and philosophy. But then what about someone who is neither religious nor poetic nor philosophically inclined? They still experience the offer of grace, Rahner would say, and their experience too must somehow or other come to symbolic expression. The logic of his position seems to drive him towards saying that absolutely anything, any element of our categorical experience whatsoever, can symbolize our experience of God's grace. And at this point one begins to wonder whether the notions of symbolizing and expressing become so stretched that they lose all their meaning.

In any case, the sacraments as usually understood, the seven sacraments, are to be seen as a special case of this universal tendency for grace to express itself in the concrete. What distinguishes them is the nature of their relationship to the Church, which I have discussed above. Rahner would say that because human beings are intrinsically social, grace and its expression always have some connection to the Church, but in the case of the sacraments the connection is at its fullest and most formal.[2]

Does this make the sacraments 'better' than other symbols? Rahner's answer is complex. On the one hand he thinks there is a kind of hierarchy of the adequacy of symbols – everything is not on the same plane. And the adequacy of the seven sacraments is in some sense of the word 'guaranteed' in a way that nothing else is. One can be absolutely sure that God's grace is really expressed and made present in them. And yet on the other hand he denies that these sacraments are in any way unique in causing grace, or that they are always more effective than other 'merely sacramental' activities. Something which is not strictly speaking a sacrament might in a particular case 'work' better in actually bringing grace home to the individual than a sacrament does.

As one might guess, Rahner has to make some subtle distinctions in order to maintain both sides of this position, in order to show that this 'on the one hand . . . on the other hand' even makes sense. This is one of the points at which a sense of strain appears in Rahner's thought. The attempt to combine a generous, sweeping and ultimately very simple vision of the way all religious experience works with an interpretation of the very specific claims of Roman Catholicism at times requires some fancy footwork, and if the footwork gets too fancy, the whole scheme can come to seem rather artificial.

5

Philosophy and Rahner's theology

A recurring hotspot for theology, at least since Tertullian asked in the third century 'What has Athens to do with Jerusalem?', has been its relationship to philosophy. This is an issue that keeps returning, a question that does not want to go away, because it is more than a mere matter of jostling between two adjacent academic disciplines: what is at stake, fundamentally, is the relationship of human wisdom, and the products of human reason, to divine revelation.

Rahner's first two books, *Spirit in the World* and *Hearer of the Word*, were works of philosophy. He was at one stage preparing for a career teaching philosophy, or at least the history of philosophy. As a student he sat at the feet (or more precisely, attended the seminars) of the most influential philosopher of the twentieth century, Martin Heidegger. And his theological writing is often saturated with philosophical terminology. The following, for example, comes from his *Foundations of Christian Faith*:

> When understood in this way, the essence and the meaning of God's self-communication to the spiritual subject consists in the fact that God becomes immediate to the subject as spiritual, that is, in the fundamental unity of knowledge and love. Ontological self-communication must be understood as the condition which makes personal and immediate knowledge and love for God possible. But this very closeness to God . . . is the real essence

of what constitutes the ontological relationship between God and creatures. (FCF 122)

Terminology of essence and accident, of subject and object, of subjectivity and objectification, of ontic and ontological, of existence and existential, of condition of the possibility, of transcendental condition of the possibility, of transcendence and transcendentality and self-transcendence, litter Rahner's prose. And they litter Rahner's prose not just in his early philosophical books, but throughout his writings. What then, in Rahner's writings, is the relation of philosophy to theology?

One answer to this question, and an answer which has seemed obvious to many, takes its cue from the order of Rahner's writings. Since Rahner's earliest major efforts were philosophical, it has seemed natural to assume that his theology is built upon this philosophy. Many have read Rahner's early books, then, as providing the basis and framework for his subsequent thought: certain truths are first established through philosophical argument, and because they have been so established, Rahner can proceed to his theology. Few suppose, of course, that everything Rahner says is simply derived from philosophy – it is hard to deny that he gives some role to revelation. But there has been quite a widely held assumption that the arguments of *Spirit in the World* and *Hearer of the Word* provide the foundation for all that follows. To some this makes Rahner particularly impressive: he has created a single, massive multi-level structure in which the philosophy serves as the starting point and justification for the theology, and it is striking in its sheer systematic coherence. For many, on the other hand, this approach has provided a reason to turn away from Rahner's work altogether: if one is not persuaded by the philosophical arguments, if one doubts that the methods employed in *Spirit in the World* and *Hearer of the Word* are legitimate, then the foundations crumble, and there is little point in reading any further.

It may be clear from the way I have presented Rahner so far that I am not inclined towards such a way of thinking. Rahner himself said various things which seem aimed at resisting this vision of his work. He liked to insist that he was not a philosopher, for instance, and at times he quite clearly distanced himself from his early writings: 'It goes without saying that today I would not always or necessarily say about certain subjects . . . what I said about them in previous years'.[1] He described *Spirit in the World* and *Hearer of the Word* as 'lopsided works of my youth', works by which he did not particularly like to be stereotyped.[2] And, as we shall see in Chapter 7, he repeatedly insisted on the eclectic and occasional nature of his work – he wrote about things as the situation demanded, and not out of any inner drive to work out a system.

I have argued at some length elsewhere[3] against seeing Rahner's philosophy as the foundation and framework for his theology. But if this is *not* the way, or at least not the best way, to see the role of philosophy in his thought, then what is?

An obvious place to go in attempting an answer to this question might seem to be Rahner's own comments about the relationship between philosophy and theology (between these two disciplines in general, that is to say, rather than between his own philosophy and his own theology). This is a theme Rahner took up on more than one occasion. Before we can explain the pattern he lays out, however, we need to go on a little detour through another topic: what Rahner has to say about philosophy and theology turns out to be parallel to, and mostly derived from, what he thinks needs saying about the topic of nature and grace. This is an issue I touched upon lightly in Chapter 2, but one which we now need to consider a little more closely.

The relationship of grace to nature has been an important issue in a great deal of Roman Catholic theology. 'Nature' in this context is used in a rather technical sense. Whereas ordinarily it refers to all that is *not* us and *not* made by us – to

mountains and plants and non-human animals – in Roman
Catholic theology 'nature' usually refers precisely to *us*, to *our*
nature, to what we are just because we are human, and indeed
to what we are capable of becoming and doing, just because
we are human. (A symphony, for example, or a computer programme, might be associated with 'the natural' in this context,
insofar as it is something which is within our natural capacities
to bring about.) Our nature is all that we are and are capable
of becoming insofar as we are created. Grace, as discussed at
some length in Chapter 2, is a gift of God which goes beyond
nature, beyond the basic gift of our being that is creation.

Exactly how to understand the relationship between nature
and grace, between what we are simply in virtue of being created, and what we may be through a further gift of grace, was
the focus of considerable controversy in the 1940s and 50s. Does
nature *need* grace? Do we already in our nature have a *desire*
for grace? Is nature in some way *incomplete* without grace? There
was felt to be a necessity both to preserve the integrity of nature,
its wholeness, so that grace really could be seen as gift and not
as something God owed – and also to see us, in our relationship to God, as integrated, and not in any way split down the
middle.

Rahner made his own contribution to this debate.[4] As we saw
in Chapter 2, he presents grace as something that is univer-
sally available to all, at all times. What this means is that there
never does in fact exist a 'pure nature', a nature untouched by
grace. There *might* have existed such a nature, in that God could
have chosen not to give himself to the world, but in fact this
is not the case. Rahner considers the concept of nature, and particularly of pure nature, to be a necessary abstraction. There
must exist a nature precisely as something which is capable of
receiving grace, and if this nature is capable of receiving grace
as grace, as free gift, it must have a certain independence. In
practice, however, nature as we find it is always already shaped
by, taken up into, grace – it is always already part of something

more than just nature. Nature, he says, is an 'inner moment' of grace.

And here we come back to the question of philosophy and theology. Philosophy, Rahner writes, is an 'inner moment' of theology. Key here is that Rahner presumes that philosophy belongs to the realm of nature, whereas theology belongs to that of grace – or to put it a little more precisely, he presumes that the subject matter of philosophy is nature, and the subject matter of theology is grace. And so, suggests Rahner, just as the nature on which philosophy reflects is an 'inner moment' of grace, so philosophy itself is an 'inner moment' of theology. Philosophy has a certain integrity, a certain independence, and it could have been that philosophy was all we had; but as a matter of fact, in this world, in the world that we actually have, the purpose of philosophy, its true goal, is to be taken up as an element into theology.

This is an interesting vision of the relationship between the two disciplines, but one that turns out in the end not to be terribly helpful – not helpful, that is, for coming to terms with the way, in Rahner's *own* writings, philosophy and theology interact. One difficulty is that it is simply too abstract, too much derived from first principles. But in addition, there is the problem that if one looks hard at it, this way of thinking about the two disciplines begins to fall apart. What Rahner does not seem to notice is that the very concepts of philosophy and theology which he is employing cease to work once the full force of his view of grace is taken into account. If he is right about grace, then the philosopher is in fact unable to avoid thinking about grace (unable, that is, to avoid doing theology). If grace is always already present to all of us, if there is no pure nature available, then there is in fact no grace-free portion of existence on which the philosopher can do his business. Although Rahner does not seem to notice this, then, on his own account of the matter the possibility of a philosophy which is not theology, of a genuine philosophy, simply disappears.

Ultimately, perhaps, it is best not to look for any very formal, theoretical account of the role of philosophy in Rahner's writings. Rahner, as it happened, was intellectually inclined towards philosophy: he tended to think in philosophical categories. It is not impossible to imagine theologians who have a leaning towards history, and are most at ease making theological points through an engagement with the past. It is, again, not impossible to imagine theologians who have literary proclivities, and reflect on incarnation or atonement with the help of discussions of novels or poems. And there are some, of course, who argue that theology really *ought* to be done primarily through literature, or that all theological arguments really *must* be historical arguments. But Rahner on the whole is not best thought of as someone driven by a belief in the importance of philosophy per se, or who puts unusual weight on its necessary role in theology: he is best understood simply as a thinker who, through a combination of circumstance and temperament, happened to think in philosophical categories. For him, philosophical concepts offered themselves as the natural idiom through which to articulate theology.

Rahner's relationship to Heidegger is, it seems to me, a case in point. Rahner attended Heidegger's seminars, and claimed to have learned something important about how to read and interpret historical texts. And he clearly took over some vocabulary from Heidegger: the term '*Vorgriff*' (p. 3), which is quite central for him, is borrowed from Heidegger, as are a number of other concepts (e.g. 'angst', 'existential', or the idea of 'thrownness'). But these are simply piecemeal, *ad hoc* borrowings, with no particular concern on Rahner's part to use them in a way that is faithful to Heidegger's programme. Those commentators who have insisted on reading Rahner as some kind of a Heideggerian have had to conclude that he was really a very bad one.

Rahner's relationship to Immanuel Kant is perhaps a little more complicated. *Spirit in the World*, Rahner's early philosophical work, shows some real grappling with Kant's thought. Because of this early engagement with Kant, Rahner is often classified as a 'transcendental Thomist'– a member of a group of Roman Catholic thinkers who attempted to interpret Thomas Aquinas through the lens of Kant. Furthermore, Rahner continued later in life to talk about the importance of a 'transcendental method' (a term that is inevitably suggestive of Kant) as one aspect of the way in which theology needs to be done. This, then, has meant that some have seen in Rahner a thorough Kantianism, so that if one does not buy into Kant's approach to philosophy, one need not deal further with Rahner's contribution to theology.

Kant was famous for inaugurating the 'turn to the subject' in philosophy. He thought that philosophy needed to answer some of its most pressing problems not by paying attention to the 'objects' around us, to the things that there are, out there in the world, so to speak, but instead by turning its attention to the mind which knows them, to the 'subject' who experiences these things. This turn to the subject is also known as the 'transcendental turn' (because what Kant thought we should pay attention to in the subject, in the knower, is not any old information we can find, but what he called the 'transcendental conditions of the possibility of experience'). One can describe Rahner, in *Spirit in the World*, as making his own 'transcendental turn'. He follows to a certain extent the same strategy as Kant, but comes to radically different conclusions. (Rahner's transcendental turn, to put it a little crudely, leads to the inescapability of knowledge of God, whereas Kant's led to its impossibility – Kant said one couldn't possibly have it, Rahner that one couldn't possibly avoid it.) And, in his theological period, Rahner continued to suggest that there was something in Kant's turn to the subject that could not be gone back on, that had to be accepted by theology as by all else.

If one looks carefully, however, at Rahner's espousal, as a theologian, of a turn to the subject, or of a transcendental method, these turn out to be a good deal more vague, and involve a good deal less commitment to a specific philosophical programme, than might at first appear. They represent in the end not so much Rahner's allegiance to a philosophical system, as a tendency to use a philosophical language to make what are in fact broad theological points. The meaningfulness of doctrines, Rahner thinks, requires that they be shown to make some sort of contact with people's experience, that their relevance can in some way be perceived. This is not a reductive insistence that theology be *derived* from experience, nor even really that theology should always be *about* experience, but that it cannot ever be presented as fundamentally *detached* from us, as really having nothing to do with us.

I am suggesting, then, that on the whole, in Rahner's later writings, philosophy functions as an idiom, a kind of language in which theology is formulated. Fundamentally, that is to say, Rahner uses philosophy to express, rather than to determine or to justify, theological positions and arguments. The distinction cannot of course be absolute. The language we use, the sets of concepts to which we turn, the ways we have of saying things, to some degree form and constrain our thought. There are inevitably aspects of Rahner's theology which are shaped, sometimes perhaps distorted, by the particular philosophical concepts with which he worked. But this philosophical influence is ultimately secondary and peripheral. The basic sources of Rahner's ideas, and the fundamental justification for them, lie elsewhere.

Before I turn, in the next chapter, to one possible view of where this 'elsewhere' might be, it is worth pausing to consider a little further one particular element of Rahner's early philosophy. In Chapter 1 I deliberately avoided tracing philosophical arguments for the notion that we all have a *Vorgriff*, a 'pre-apprehension of Being' which is also a pre-apprehension of God. I suggested then that I (and many others) do not consider them successful, but also that I do not think they are crucial for Rahner's theology. Nevertheless, some readers may be left curious: this seems such a central feature of his thought, and at the same time, considered philosophically at least, such an outrageous claim. How did Rahner in fact think it could be established?

The first thing to note here is that nowhere does Rahner actually set out a simple, rigorous argument which is supposed to prove to all comers that they have this *Vorgriff,* this constant awareness of being and God. The question is dealt with originally in *Spirit in the World,* and it is from here that one can abstract the fullest version of an argument. But *Spirit in the World* is not written as an abstract piece of philosophy of religion for general consumption – it is written as an interpretation of a particular aspect of the thought of Thomas Aquinas. The interpretation of Aquinas becomes, it is true, a platform from which Rahner works out his own position; nevertheless, the whole ambience of the book is one in which the existence of God is never in question. The argument laid out for the *Vorgriff* in *Spirit in the World* is not in any sense an argument written with unbelievers in mind.

The line of reasoning in *Spirit in the World* trades, as do some more informal sketches of arguments Rahner develops elsewhere, on the relationship between limitation and unlimitedness. The key notion is that one can only recognize limit against some broader, limitless, background.

In *Spirit in the World,* Rahner's focus is on the making of judgements, such as 'This is a desk' or 'This is a wolf'. In any such judgement, one is applying a universal concept to a particular thing: to say 'This is a desk' or 'This is a wolf' is to see this particular as belonging to the general category of desks or wolves. And this is possible only if one can see something in this particular desk – call it, following a philosophical tradition that goes back to Plato and Aristotle, the 'form' of the desk – which could also be found in other desks. According to Rahner, this in turn is possible only if one sees the form of the desk or the wolf as somehow *limited* by the particular stuff, the matter, of this desk or this wolf. So making judgements involves using universal concepts, but we cannot use such concepts without recognizing matter as limiting form. The next step is to ask, how are we *able* to recognize matter as limiting form? This, says Rahner, could not happen unless we had at the same time an awareness of a broader field of possibilities for the form – and this is the *Vorgriff*. Through an argument that I will not detail here, but which draws on the fact that when we make judgements we are affirming something, not just about our concepts, but about the way things are in themselves, he arrives at the conclusion that this broader field of possibilities can only be Being as such.

For most readers this argument, or the part of it that I have outlined, is likely to seem rather alien: language of form and matter is not second nature to most of us, and even less so the notion of form as somehow limited by matter. It needs to be said again that Rahner produced this argument in a specific context: it is internal to a very particular Thomistic philosophical tradition. Even if one looks at it on its own terms, however – even if one can somehow take on board the whole apparatus Rahner here uses – I think (and have tried to show elsewhere[5]) that the argument is far from workable.

It is telling, of course, that Rahner seemed to feel no need to set out formally an equivalent argument *outside* the context of this highly technical Thomism – something we might expect to be a priority if he is wanting or hoping to convince all comers of their implicit belief in God. He did however sometimes hint at a less technical style of argument. That the human being transcends the finite, that we go beyond the world of the senses, towards something more, that we are permanently open to, orientated towards, the infinite – these are things, Rahner sometimes suggests, we can see to be true because of what happens if we try to deny them. If we try to say the opposite, he maintains, we cannot avoid implicitly contradicting ourselves.

I cannot say 'I am limited to what is finite' without silently presupposing infinity – how would I even know what it *means* to be finite without contrasting this with an infinite horizon? What would it mean to suppose my thinking, or my experiencing, to be fundamentally limited and constrained, if I did not have some perception, some dim awareness at least, of unlimitedness?

There is an analogy to be drawn, Rahner sometimes suggests, with the situation of the person who affirms quite definitely that there is no truth. In the very affirming of the proposition 'there is no truth', she is in fact asserting a truth: she falls, then, into what is sometimes called 'performative self-contradiction'. Rahner thinks the same kind of thing is involved in insisting that one's knowing or awareness are essentially circumscribed: one cannot insist on this without implicitly pre-supposing, and in some way being in touch with, something which exceeds these limits. One cannot speak of a limit without already affirming something lying beyond the limit. In the very act of insisting on the limit, one goes beyond it, one transcends it.

There are of course a number of ways in which one might want to criticize such arguments. Should we perhaps distinguish between *imagining* the 'beyond' of a limit (which is perhaps unavoidable), and actually having an *awareness* of something beyond a limit (which perhaps does not happen)? And even if this is not a problem, is there not a leap going on here, from noticing that no particular limit to our experience can be named, to the conclusion that we have some actual experience of unlimitedness? Is this in some way akin to a move from 'There is no limit to how big numbers can get' to 'There is some unlimitedly big number'?

What must again be stressed here is the fact that Rahner did not pursue this kind of question in any great detail or with any particular anxiety. From time to time he made suggestions along the lines I have described, but he never really tried to construct an argument with sufficient care that it might withstand the sceptical questions which would inevitably be raised by an atheist. Rather than attempting to place himself on neutral ground from which he might persuade unbelievers, Rahner is best understood as articulating in a philosophical idiom something that was part of his general theological vision, namely a sense of the utter inescapability of God.

6

Spirituality and Rahner's theology

Rahner worked as a professional theologian, teaching students, writing articles and books, giving lectures, putting forward proposals, making arguments, developing new interpretations of ancient concepts, and so on. But he also preached, led retreats, and published prayers. On the face of it sermons, prayers and talks in retreats are rather different from academic theology. It would be easy to suppose that an academic theologian who engages in spiritual writings does this on the side, as a kind of pious hobby; one might think that he speaks from some different part of himself, leaving behind the complex issues with which he wrestles in the office, or at most tossing in a few titbits of learning by way of illustration. In Rahner's case it is not, however, at all like this: though the two are clearly different – the prayers, for instance, sound like prayers and not like scholarship – they are nevertheless organically connected. At times, indeed, it is in his spiritual writings, and his writings on spirituality, that the fundamental impetus and direction of Rahner's theology becomes most clear.

One way to approach the relationship between Rahner's theology and his spiritual writings is to look at the way some of the themes considered in previous chapters emerge in Rahner's published prayers. In Chapter 1, for instance, I discussed his vision of humanity as always transcending itself towards God, always somehow experiencing God in all our ordinary experiences. This same vision frequently animates Rahner's prayers, so that praying itself becomes an acknowledgement, a remembering, of the utter inescapability of God:

> I'm constantly tempted to creep away from You in utter discouragement, back to the things that are more comprehensible, to things with which my heart feels so much more at home than it does with Your mysteriousness.
>
> And yet, where shall I go? If the narrow hut of this earthly life with its dear, familiar trivialities, its joys and sorrows both great and small – if this were my real home, wouldn't it still be surrounded by Your distant Endlessness? Could the earth be my home without Your far-away heaven above it? . . .
>
> Without you, I should founder helplessly in my own dull and groping narrowness. I could never feel the pain of longing, not even deliberately resign myself to being content with this world, had not my mind again and again soared out over its own limitations into the hushed reaches which are filled by You alone, the Silent Infinite. Where should I flee before You, when all my yearning for the unbounded, even my bold trust in my littleness, is really a confession of You? (ES 6–7)

This sense of God's presence at the heart of human life constantly comes back in Rahner's spiritual writings as it does in his theology. But what is more unmissable in the prayers than it is in Rahner's strictly academic writing is that his insistence on God's immediacy to us is not tied up with any superficial cheerfulness about human life. The passage above begins with a sense of difficulty and discouragement, with a desire to creep away, and this is quite typical. In another prayer from the same collection, Rahner writes about God's relationship to our daily routine, the daily drudgery of existence.[1] He evokes a sense of the everyday as one of endless, scattered tedium:

In Your loving mercy, look at my soul, a road crowded
by a dense and endless column of bedraggled refugees,
a bomb-pocked highway on which countless trivialities,
much empty talk and pointless activity, idle curiosity and
ludicrous pretensions of importance all roll forward in a
never-ending stream. (ES 45)

His soul, he writes,

has become a huge warehouse where day after day the trucks
unload their crates without any plan or discrimination,
to be piled helter-skelter in every corner and cranny, until
it is crammed full from top to bottom with the trite, the
commonplace, the insignificant, the routine. (ES 46)

And Rahner's prayer suggests that one does not escape all this
even in religious activity, in prayer or contemplation or the saying of mass: he raises the possibility of becoming a Carthusian
(a member of a silent, contemplative religious order), but con-
cludes that this would not solve the problem, 'since not even
the sacred actions I now perform are free from the corrosive dust
of this spirit of routine' (ES 47–8). All of our life is routine, all
becomes a kind of drudgery, even what we do on a Sunday:
'*Every* day is "everyday"' (ES 49). If God is to be found at all,
it is not by an escape into something more pure, elevated or
special, but somehow in the midst of this everyday ordinariness.

Rahner is usually seen as a fundamentally optimistic theologian, and this is in one sense perfectly right. He believes in
the universal availability of grace, the universal possibility of
salvation, and he refuses to give to sin an absolutely fundamental
role in driving salvation history. But what becomes clear in
such prayers is that the optimism is not borne of superficial
'positive thinking'. Rahner's spiritual writings are marked by
an honesty that refuses any kind of escapism, that refuses to
be spiritual by romanticizing or glossing over the ordinary, by
ignoring or simply turning away from what is boring, shabby,

pathetic or stifling.[2] Again and again one finds Rahner returning to the reality in which we actually find ourselves, and rooting his prayers and meditations here. There is a vast sweep to
Rahner's thought, a real speculative boldness, but at the same
time a constant attention to and return to the mundane: it is
completely in character that in 1964 he published a series of
meditations, *Everyday Things*, reflecting theologically on such
topics as working, sitting, moving, seeing, sleeping, laughing and
eating.

Both this insistence on rooting spirituality in ordinary and
unimpressive reality, and something of the rationale for it, are
particularly clear in one of Rahner's published retreat talks. Here,
as a preamble to the retreat, Rahner warns of the danger of too
much piety that forgets our ordinary selves: there is a danger,
he writes, that we

> jump ahead of our own reality. Then it can happen that
> a person prays, makes resolutions, sighs for the everlast-
> ing hills, and in the whole process falls into the illusion
> that the 'old man' is no longer present and thinks that he
> will not return for some time. (SE 13)

Such an approach, Rahner implies, is likely to prove infertile, so
that 'everything is the same after the retreat as it was before'.
The explanation he suggests for this is telling: it may just be
that 'the "old man" was not invited to come along and make
the retreat' (SE 13). There is in the end, in other words, no point
at all in forms of piety that leave our unimpressive and humdrum real selves behind.

Alongside his sometimes almost depressive psychological
realism, and alongside the recurring sense of the inescapability of God, another common theme in Rahner's prayers
and writings on prayer is a sense of wonder, of astonishment,
at the very fact that we *can* pray, that we can dare to address
God at all. This is not obvious, not to be taken for granted,
but is in Rahner's presentation profoundly startling. He writes

with some sympathy of those who suppose prayer to be impossible: if God, the 'all-overwhelming and incomprehensible mystery', cannot be made into an object, then surely this mystery cannot be addressed as a You, cannot be spoken to. Rahner does not in the end agree with this – the fact that we do pray and that we must pray is, for him, non-negotiable. But this very fact – 'That the creature can "treat" with his creator . . . can "do business" with his Ground' (PF 85) – is one that ought not to seem obvious, that cannot be taken lightly. It is, Rahner says, 'the very loftiest thing one can say about man', and both his written prayers and his reflections on prayer convey the sense that there is something paradoxical and in fact shocking here.

Note that what is startling for Rahner is *not* simply that we have an awareness of God, that God is the ever-present horizon of our lives. Although we may overlook it, this is, on his view, obvious and impossible to question. What is paradoxical, what is astonishing, is rather the fact that we can *pray to* this mystery, that we can *address* this 'horizon'. Now, in Chapter 2 we saw that, in addition to a universal awareness of God as horizon, Rahner maintains that we all have an experience of grace, an experience in which 'the horizon draws near' and gives itself to us. We saw, in other words, that Rahner believes not only in a universal natural awareness of God, but in a universal experience of something which goes beyond our nature, a universal experience of God's self-communication. Rahner's sense of the wonder of the fact that we can pray at all, that we can, so to speak, 'tap God on the shoulder', is fundamentally connected to the notion that God's self-communication to us is truly a matter of grace, something freely given, not to be taken for granted. For it is only because God has drawn near and given himself to us that we have the possibility of turning in prayer to him.

Rahner's prayers, then, often exhibit the same themes that his articles and books centre upon, and sometimes in the prayers an important light is shed on his theology. But if we stopped with this observation we would be missing something important. Rahner was not just a theologian who also wrote spiritual materials, nor even a theologian who was also a priest who wrote spiritual materials. He was more specifically a Jesuit, a member of the religious order founded by Ignatius of Loyola. Another important way to approach this topic, then, is to examine Rahner's theological writings on specifically 'Ignatian' themes, and so to consider the relation of his theology to Ignatian spirituality.

Rahner repeatedly pointed, especially late in life, to the importance of Ignatius, and of his own formation as a Jesuit, in the shaping of his thought. He suggested that Ignatius might in fact be a more important influence on him than any of the major philosophers or theologians of the tradition. And more generally he insisted that the works of Ignatius, though they do not display any intellectual sophistication, are of deep importance for theology – Ignatius' writings are not a kind of derivative, second-rate or second-hand theology, but something more fundamental than any academic theology, something which theology has to ponder, try to understand and catch up with. They are, he presumes, an important *source* for theological reflection, and a source that has not yet been adequately explored.

Rahner himself took up, at one time or another, a variety of themes from Ignatius and the Ignatian tradition in order to reflect on them theologically. He wrote about the notion of a 'consolation without cause' and Ignatius' understanding of discernment, about the notion of finding God in all things and the Jesuit motto '*ad maiorem Dei gloriam*' ('to the greater glory of God'), about the ideal of contemplation in action and about the concept of indifference. It would be quite possible, of course, to relegate such themes as discernment, indifference, or Ignatius' notions of consolation and desolation to the realm of the practical, to the realm of things that spiritual directors need to concern themselves with, to see them as important psychologically and spiritually but nevertheless quite different from the more hard-core stuff that it is the business of theologians to reflect on. But, once again, for Rahner it is not like this. He presumes that central Ignatian concepts are theologically important, that they carry a real theological weight, and that they require real theological reflection.

Consider, for instance, the notion of 'indifference'. Ignatius wrote that we need 'to make ourselves indifferent to all created things' so that 'we want not health rather than sickness, riches rather than poverty, honour rather than dishonour, long rather than short life': we need to cultivate indifference so that we will want only what leads to God's glory and our salvation, so that we will desire and choose 'only what is most conducive for us to the end for which we are created'.[3] We have to strive to free ourselves from too great an attachment to any particular created being or to any particular created state of affairs.

Rahner relates this indifference, first of all, to his understanding of human transcendence, to his concept of human nature, that is to say, outlined in Chapter 1, according to which we are by nature constantly transcending all things towards God.

> For if man is always the one who grasps the finite, individual thing in his knowledge and in his freedom in a movement directed basically towards absolute reality, towards absolute truth and goodness, in the necessary realization of his mental life he always transcends the individual thing, he dissociates himself from it, he sets the finite, individual thing against a broader horizon, he rises above it, makes himself independent of it: he is 'indifferent' in regard to the individual thing. (PF 214)

Indifference, in other words, is built into the very way we are, the way our minds inescapably work.

On the face of it this assertion that we are *already* indifferent seems quite odd in light of Ignatius' presentation of indifference as a thing we must aim at and strive for, something we must cultivate and work towards. But Rahner goes on to insist that the way that we are is *also* in another sense something to be achieved, something we must work to bring about – 'The indifference of our nature is the essential task of our life, it has to be undertaken . . . we must want to be the transcendence that we are' (PF 215). What does this mean? Rahner suggests that we are always tempted to take some finite thing and suppose that this alone is what will make us really happy and fulfilled. We do inevitably transcend all things towards God, but we don't want to do this, we for some reason resist what we are by nature:

> We are constantly under the impression . . . that some particular thing in our life would make us free, exhilarated, blissfully happy; we are continually identifying ourselves with some particular thing, we don't want to transcend this, to get away from it and sacrifice it. (PF 216)

It is perhaps worth noting at this point that neither on Rahner's account, nor on that of most interpreters of the Ignatian tradition, does this indifference require that one be cold and unfeeling toward everything that comes one's way, that one enjoy nothing and love no one. Rahner is clear that finite, created things are good and 'willed by God', the work of a good creator, and so ought to be 'affirmed, accepted, enjoyed and loved by us'. It is the latching on to things, the instinct to base ourselves on, to stop with, particular created goods that is the problem.

This instinct to resist our own transcendence, to hold on for our happiness to finite things, is presented by Rahner as fundamentally sinful, but also as something to be found in all of us. The business of becoming indifferent is then the task of constantly overcoming this instinct, and it is not a light task: the overcoming can occur 'only painfully and through the experience of something like death' (PF 215). What is required in indifference is that we turn from what we understand to the incomprehensible, from what we are enjoying to what is promised, from the present to the future, from what we can grasp to what we cannot grasp. (PF 216)

Furthermore, it is not something we can do once and for all, for we constantly come across different things which we want to latch on to and identify ourselves with, and which we are constantly in need of 'surmounting': becoming indifferent is 'a task freshly imposed each day', part of the 'daily dying with Christ'.

What, fundamentally, is accomplished in Rahner's treatment of indifference? On the one hand, it becomes clear here that his insistence on humanity's transcendence, on the fact that we all always go beyond all finite things towards God, is not a basis for complacency, for a relaxed sense that everything necessary is already accomplished. The treatment of indifference makes it clear that in Rahner's eyes, although transcendence is indeed always already given, it is in fact always already what we are, it is not *just* a given, not *just* something we already have or are. It needs to be embraced, and the embracing of it is the arduous task of the whole of a Christian life. Once again, then, Rahner's discussion of a theme from spirituality sheds important light on a central theme of his theology.

On the other hand, the fact that Rahner discusses this theme from spirituality in the context of his fundamental theological vision of the human being means that indifference itself is cast in a particular light. On Rahner's account, indifference, though it may, perhaps must, go against our sinful tendencies, does not run contrary to our most basic nature, but with it; it is not ultimately a demand posed from outside, arbitrarily placed on us. It is not a peculiar, special thing only to be attempted by those who want to be Jesuits. Rahner integrates indifference into a much larger vision, so that it comes to seem not an extrinsically imposed demand, but an intrinsic requirement of what it is to be human. Difficult though it may be, on some level to strive for indifference is to go with the grain of what we are, rather than against it, to fulfil rather than to frustrate ourselves.

So far in this chapter I have traced various connections between Rahner's strictly theological writings and his spiritual writings. It should have become clear by now that when Rahner writes in these two different areas, there is a certain unity and integrity to his thought that overrides conventional divides. But a final question we might ask is, which side of his work should we consider to be primary? Which aspect is it that drives the other?

An obvious possibility might be to presume that Rahner develops his theological ideas first, and then applies them in prayers and spiritual writing, translating them into this more devotional or practical genre. He takes ideas that he has already worked out, one might think, and uses them to interpret Ignatian concepts, to guide the way he runs retreats, to give content and form to his prayers.

One weakness of such an interpretation is that it does not seem to take into account Rahner's comments, mentioned above, about the importance of Ignatian spirituality in shaping his own thought. Nor does it sit well with what he says about the proper relationship between academic theology and a spiritual text of the kind Ignatius left behind. Quite a different way of looking at Rahner has been suggested recently in a carefully argued book by Philip Endean, SJ, entitled *Karl Rahner and Ignatian Spirituality*. Endean takes the notion of an immediate experience of God to be a touchstone for Rahner's thought, the thing which most distinctively shapes his theology, the point from which his most creative ideas emerge. The influence of Ignatius on Rahner is in the very fact of this centrality: Rahner is showing his Ignatian roots in this insistence that an immediate experience of God is fundamental to Christianity. The *shape* of Rahner's understanding of this immediate experience, however, should not be traced so much to Ignatius as to Rahner's study of figures such as Bonaventure (1217–74), Evagrius (346–99) and Gregory of Nyssa (330–95). Endean makes the fascinating suggestion that Rahner takes over from such thinkers a description of an extremely rare mystical state, an experience which on their account is very occasionally granted to those far advanced in the contemplative life, and uses this to develop a theology of a *universal* experience of grace. Rahner drew from this mystical tradition, that is to say, the notion of an apprehension of God in darkness, an experience of the obscure but immediate 'touch' of God, and developed it into a whole theology of grace. In the last chapter I suggested that it would be a mistake to see Rahner's theology as controlled or determined by a philosophical position. If Endean is right, then one can perhaps instead see Rahner's theology as ultimately driven by, and rooted in, spirituality.[4]

Of course, people are complex, and so too is the development of their thinking. The range and variety of Rahner's work is enormous (something I shall pick up in the next chapter). It is perhaps unnecessary to settle on any particular account of which aspect of Rahner's thought 'comes first', so to speak, or to single out any one element that drives all the rest.[5] What is particularly useful in Endean's proposal is that it can shake us out of any tendency to suppose that the 'spiritual' must, intellectually, be secondary to 'real' theology.

It has become commonplace in recent theological literature to regret the divide that has arisen between spirituality and theology, to bemoan the loss of unity between them. The source of regret here is not that theologians are not sufficiently spiritual as individuals – no doubt some of them are. The problem is that theology as such has ceased to be seen as connected to the actual leading of a Christian life. And the other side of this is that when people do want to say something about how to lead a Christian life, it does not occur to them that they need to be doing theology. What I have suggested in this chapter is not that Rahner as an individual was very spiritual and integrated – he may well have been, of course, but then this is no doubt also true of many a second-rate and misguided theologian – but that he did theology in a way that was not divided from an articulation of, and a reflection on, the spiritual life. He did not generally go out of his way to announce that this was what he was doing, nor did he, like Hans Urs von Balthasar, describe his work as a 'kneeling theology'. But when one begins to look at what he does, at the connections between his academic work and his spiritual writings, at the range of issues that concern him in his more speculative theology, and at the sources of his inspiration, then an unusual level of integrity between the spiritual and the theological emerges.

7

Rahner the dilettante

Many of the themes I have explored so far have been rather closely linked. Rahner's understanding of human nature, Christ, grace, the Church and the sacraments are all to one degree or another interrelated. The relationships are complex and not always tidy, and over the years there are certain changes in Rahner's tone and emphasis. But there is nevertheless something like a systematic core to Rahner's thought, a core which includes the topics we have so far discussed and a few others (for instance, his treatment of the doctrine of the Trinity). And in the last chapter we saw how such interrelated theological themes are also integrally connected to Rahner's spiritual writings.

The systematic aspect of Rahner's theology has attracted much attention and enthusiasm among his admirers, and a great deal of ink has been spilled trying to work out more precisely than Rahner himself did how everything fits together. But though this can be a fascinating business, it would be a mistake, and very unfair to Rahner's thought, to think of it as *nothing but* a tightly interlocking system of a few ideas. In fact Rahner's thought is much richer and more intriguing than this, and provides much of value even to those who are not drawn to its systematic core.

There are two reasons for this. First, even when Rahner writes on one of the central themes mentioned above, he is prone to make observations and suggestions along the way which are not bound up with these core elements of his thought, and which are often fascinating in themselves. This means that those who might reject outright his conclusions can nevertheless find much worth pondering in his arguments. So for instance a range of contemporary theologians may accept and find interesting the suggestion mentioned in Chapter 2 about 'closet docetism' (the suggestion, that is, that many apparently orthodox Christians in fact give only lip-service to the idea of Christ's full humanity) without going on to adopt Rahner's own way of understanding the humanity and divinity of Christ.

Secondly, there is the sheer breadth of Rahner's writings. Though Rahner's thought has a kind of centre – a few interlocking themes to which he returns again and again – there is a good deal more to it than this. On the whole, Rahner chose not to produce large systematic works of theology, but instead to write hundreds and hundreds of brief essays, and this gave him the freedom to explore a vast range of topics. Rahner liked to describe himself as a dilettante, and this was not sheer modesty. Browsing through his works one can come across essays on the theology of power and the theology of leisure and the theology of childhood; on poetry; on nuclear disarmament; on anxiety; on the angels, on indulgences and on Mary; on the televising of masses; on the diaconate; on the pope in relation to the bishops; on devotion to the saints and devotion to the sacred heart of Jesus; on the relationship between Christianity and Marxism, between Christianity and evolutionary theory, between Christianity and psychotherapy. And so on.

It would clearly be futile to try to summarize the whole range of themes on which Rahner wrote, but a brief sampling of an arbitrary selection of these may help to make it clear that there is more to Rahner's thought than a single 'system', and it may give the reader a taste for browsing through the many volumes of his *Theological Investigations*.

Pluralism

In his middle age Rahner begins to write about how the intellectual world has become something radically different from the one which he and his colleagues knew in their youth, during the period of their own intellectual training. What he is referring to is not a change in beliefs, a switch from one philosophy to another, say, or from one dominant strand of theology to another. It is not a matter of one group of intellectuals gaining ascendancy over another. The difference is deeper and more troubling than this. In his youth things seemed manageable; now, they are no longer so. The intellectual world with all its specializations and divisions has expanded dramatically, and as a result there is, quite simply, too much to know. This means that the ideal of the 'renaissance man', of the person who is equally competent in all different areas of human knowledge and accomplishment, is no longer attainable. But it means a good deal more than that. Even if one wants to specialize in a single area – in, say, theology – it is no longer possible, Rahner thinks, to master all the things that one should know.

Theology always, by Rahner's account, makes use of philosophy. And so in principle the theologian ought to sort through all the philosophies there have been and come up with her own synthesis, rejecting what is wrong while taking from each the good points and the genuine insights. And in his youth, this is what Rahner thought he was doing (or so he later suggests. See TI XIII 71). But he comes to believe that there are in fact so many schools and styles of philosophy, and so many problems within philosophy, that no one thinker can ever really get to the point of fully understanding and appreciating them all, and so nobody can be in a position to sift and judge them and create a synthesis which fully takes into account everything which has gone before.

Some philosophers have recently played with the idea that different systems of thought can be 'incommensurable'. This would mean, roughly, that there can be no translating between one system and another, and so no comparisons and no possibility of making judgements between them. Meaning and truth become relative to the system within which one operates, because there is no moving between systems. It is interesting to note that although Rahner does not adopt any such notion of incommensurability, in practice his position leads to a rather similar view of our intellectual situation. Rahner is not a relativist. Indeed, he tends to assume that in principle it is possible to judge between different systems, different philosophies, different claims to truth. But because there is this tremendous 'pluralism' of systems and philosophies, and because the pluralism is more than any individual can master (it is an 'irreducible' pluralism), we cannot *in practice* make such judgements, or rather we cannot make enough of them to rise above the pluralism, and so we might as well be living in a world of incommensurable systems.

Our new intellectual situation is not a problem just for academics – to some degree it affects everyone. Think, for example, of all the questions that ought to be gone into in order for a person to decide whether Christian belief is intellectually justified. One ought in principle to be up to date with the ins and outs of the latest biblical scholarship so as to be in a position to make a judgement about how historically credible central Christian claims are. One ought to make a profound study of all the world religions (and non-religious systems) so as to understand the alternatives to Christian faith. One ought to study the psychology of religious experience and examine what the sociologists have to say about how we form our beliefs. One ought to examine the latest theories of the physicists and biologists. And so on. One ought to do all these things, but there is not in fact time for any one person, in a single lifetime, to do them, even if such a person had no other calls upon their energy. The problem is not unique to Christianity. How can one in general, Rahner asks, responsibly make a decision for, or responsibly hold, any world-view if one cannot possibly in a lifetime come to grips with all the questions and all the information directly relevant to holding this world-view?

This is a topic on which Rahner poses a lot of questions, and only begins to hint at a few answers. The really important thing, he thinks, is that theologians should realize that we are in this situation of intellectual pluralism, that the situation will not go away again and cannot be overcome by greater and greater efforts, and that they should begin to reflect on what this means for theology, for the Church and for Christian faith. As regards the question of how someone can intellectually justify her faith, Rahner suggests that because the obvious, 'direct' method is impossible there must be some other, 'indirect' method. He does not commit himself too far on what exactly this indirect method might be, but seems to hint that it involves taking into account, far more than is usually supposed, the *particular* situation of the individual in question.

Heresy

Heresy is something which one might perhaps not expect a modern theologian to dwell on. It seems an outdated concept, and one contemporary Christians might hope to forget, given the overtones it carries of intolerance, fanaticism, witch-hunting, burning at the stake and so on. Rahner, however, takes it up in one of his many short pieces. Why, he asks, has there been throughout Christian history such a visceral, emotional response to heresy or supposed heresy, and why has this now become so foreign? And what role, if any, does the idea of heresy have to play in our contemporary view of the Church?

The first question, then, is this: how can we make intelligible to ourselves the Christian history of extreme reaction to heresy, the history which includes the Inquisition and religious wars and the like? We may not want to approve of or defend these things, but how can we even make sense of their prominent place in the history of Christianity? A variety of factors have contributed to this violent history, Rahner suggests, but part of the explanation must be that in Christianity truth, a particular kind of truth revealed by God, has always been understood as intrinsically linked to salvation. To lose it, to distort it, is fundamentally to destroy oneself. And the heretic is one who grasps the truth, but then distorts and destroys it.

The reason that we now find Christianity's traditional reaction to heresy so foreign is that a very different attitude towards truth, especially truth in religious matters, has come to prevail in the modern world. We tend to think that in such questions 'on democratic principles every opinion has equal rights' (OH 12). Well-meaning people acting in good conscience come to all sorts of different conclusions. Therefore, it seems to us, it cannot really, fundamentally matter whether one gets it right or not:

> Knowledge of truth ... has, therefore, moved from the centre of human existence to its periphery. It belongs with things like colour of the hair, taste, race, on which a man's absolute value cannot be made to depend. (OH 11)

Rahner considers this contemporary attitude towards truth unacceptable for a Christian. Without wanting to instigate a return to religious violence, then, he is willing to suggest that the fundamental understanding of truth which made possible a violent response to heresy is in fact the right one.

If Rahner is going to take such a hard-line view, one could ask, what happens to the possibility of salvation for non-Christians? If knowing the truth is so vitally important, does this mean that non-believers are just up the creek? One might wonder, in other words, how Rahner can square this sort of position on truth with his apparently much more generous theory of anonymous Christianity. As is so often the case with Rahner, the distinction between explicit and implicit levels of consciousness, between what goes on in the depths and what is made explicit on the surface of consciousness, comes to the rescue:

> in certain circumstances a person may ... be able to arrive at and affirm a truth, precisely as truth, in the depths of his actual accomplishment of life, even when he thinks

himself obliged to deny it in his consciously formulated concepts, or knows nothing of it explicitly. (OH 16)

So, for example,

> there can be people who consider themselves atheists whilst in truth they affirm God, for example by unconditional dedication to an honest search for truth, or by fidelity to the absolute judgement of conscience . . . (OH 16)

Rahner's view, then, is not what he describes as the usual modern one, namely that if a person is well-meaning and acting in good conscience *it does not matter* whether she has latched on to the truth or not. Instead he maintains that if a person is well-meaning and acting in good conscience she has *in fact* latched on to the truth, whether she appears to have done so or not. In this way he can reconcile the traditional view that truth (and therefore heresy) is a serious matter, with the modern conviction that one cannot simply condemn everyone who holds different opinions.

Does all this mean that Christians should once again start heresy hunting? Yes and no. Truth, and therefore heresy, still matter. But heresy in the modern Church tends to take a different shape than it has traditionally done. It is now more likely to be 'latent' and hidden. One reason is that the general intellectual situation is altered. As we saw in the previous section, Rahner thinks that in recent times there has been an enormous expansion in our intellectual world, an explosion in the amount of information, ideas, theories and experiences which impinge upon us.

We cannot master it all. On the other hand we cannot simply ignore it and say it has nothing to do with us. All these things contribute to making up the mental world within which we live, the intellectual climate in which we function. We do not each construct our own system of beliefs and our own way of looking at the world, but at least in part we pick these things up from the society around us. We absorb things from a wider intellectual world which we do not control, and we may not even be aware of this process of absorption. And at least some of what we pick up is likely to be at odds with the Christian faith. So the 'orthodox Christian', who explicitly professes every-thing that the Church teaches, is bound to have at the same time other ideas and ideals, acquired without deliberate choice from the wider mental world in which we all live, and so she may well, without actually realizing it, be to one degree or another a heretic. There is in addition a second reason, specific to Roman Catholicism, for the changing shape of heresy: as the teaching authority of the Church has become more formalized (in the nineteenth-century declaration of papal infallibility, for instance) there has been less room for manoeuvre on an explicit level. Heresy has had, therefore, to go underground.

A latent heresy, by Rahner's account, is very often a heresy of emphasis. One remains verbally orthodox. One does not deny anything that is official church teaching. But one pays atten-tion to what one likes, and ignores what one does not. Now, it is impossible to work out in theory a way of determining what counts as such a heresy, for the question of emphasis is intrinsically an elusive one. Who is to say, asks Rahner, intro-ducing a rather unexpected example,

> at what point present-day sport and athletics start to become an unavowed heresy altering the due proportions and relation between personality and body, a heresy of tacit idolatry of the physical? (OH 65)

And even if one did suggest that there was such a heresy about, one could make no impact:

> every adherent of the heresy [if it is in fact a heresy] considers that it is simply others who are meant, who are indulging in such idolatry even more one-sidedly and radically. (OH 65)

One might regard this idea that heresy can be latent as rather a frightening one. Now the witch-hunt can really begin, since anyone, no matter what they say, may be a hidden heretic. Rahner thinks, however, that one should draw the opposite sort of conclusion. Hidden heresies of the kind he describes cannot be combated by the church authorities. All that the authorities can do is to issue general warnings which everyone will think applies to someone else. To the degree that heresies are latent, then, they must become primarily a matter for the individual judgement and the individual conscience. And because even those who want to be and believe themselves to be 'good Catholics' can in fact be heretics, heresy must come to be understood not as something hated and alien with which one labels the other, but as a possibility threatening all who want to be Christians equally. Rather than shifting the conservative, 'orthodox' elements in the Church back towards witch-hunts, then, Rahner is hoping to shift them away from self-satisfied complacency.

Death

Death gives meaning to our lives. This sounds like a perverse and rather grim thing to suggest, but imagine an existence without death. If our lives went on and on for ever, suggests Rahner, nothing that we did would have any particular significance, because everything could later be undone – all our mistakes one day rectified, all our good deeds eventually undermined, all our decisions later reversed. True freedom, Rahner maintains, is

> not the power constantly to change one's course of action, but rather the power to decide that which is to be final and definitive in one's life, that which cannot be superseded or replaced, the power to bring into being from one's own resources that which must be, and must not pass away, the summons to a decision that is irrevocable. (TI VII 287)

Without this possibility of making a once-and-for-all decision we could have only 'a miserable sort of freedom, condemned,
as it were, to proceed in futile circles without any final resting
place, ultimately meaningless' (TI VII 287). Because our lives
have an end-point, a limit, because we have only a finite span,
everything that we do has a reality, an intensity and a significance that would otherwise be lacking.

Death is not, however, by Rahner's account, *only* the end-point,
the limit of life. It is also to be understood as something we
are experiencing throughout our lives, a process which permeates
human existence. Constantly over the years we are reminded
of our finiteness, our limitations, our lack of control. We suffer;
we fail; we lose what we have become attached to. Even if all
goes ideally well, we cannot remain for ever in a particular phase
of our life, but have to give up one situation in order to move
on to the next. Eventually we grow old and lose our energy and
our faculties. All these things are, Rahner suggests, part of the
one process of dying which simply reaches its end and cul-
mination in the actual biological event of death, when 'every
power, down to the last vestige of a possibility, of autonom-
ously controlling his own destiny, is taken from [a person]'
(TI VII 290). The proper response, in Rahner's view, to this loss
of control, to this constant dying and finally death, is acceptance
in faith. We do not freely control our own fate, but we have a
freedom – and this Rahner takes to be our ultimate and most
important freedom – to accept this lack of control or to rebel
against it. This does not mean that we must deliberately give
up the powers that we have, or give in to an illness and drift
off into death without a struggle. The good things in life, and
our own health and powers, are indeed good, and to be appreciated. But when we really do encounter our limits and our
powerlessness, we meet a kind of invitation to recognize that
none of these are the final, the ultimate, the absolute good, and
that we must not hold on to them as if they were. And so in
death and in the dying that goes on throughout life, we have a

choice – indeed Rahner regards it as our most fundamental choice. We can accept our lack of control over ourselves and our world, and put our trust and our hope in God, or else rebel, cling to our own powers and ultimately despair.

If this is death, what becomes of life after death? 'After' is a worrying word in this context, since it seems to suggest a continuation in time after death. Rahner insists that the Christian teaching about eternal life should not be understood in this way, as though 'we only change horses and then ride on' (FCF 436, quoting Feuerbach). To conceive of it along these lines would in fact amount, he thinks, to trying to escape the reality of death, and it would undermine the real seriousness of our one, limited life-span. We can talk about eternal life, but eternity must be understood as something *contrasted* to time, and not as time stretching on for ever.

Rahner is very clear, then, about what picture of life 'after' death must be rejected. But what picture should we put in its place? This is not so clear. Rahner writes about experiencing eternity in time in various ways, particularly in the experience of freedom and responsibility. So we might suppose that, like a variety of other contemporary thinkers, he is in fact denying that there is anything beyond this life – eternity refers perhaps to a certain *quality* in our lives here and now. But this would be too simple, for Rahner also writes about the Christian *hope* that our lives will find their consummation and fulfilment in an 'absolute nearness to God', with the implication that such a fulfilment can occur in 'eternity' and not in our lives as we already know them. Rahner clearly rejects the idea that there is nothing but the life of here and now. But then when exactly, we might ask, is this consummation and fulfilment of our lives going to happen, if neither in the here and now nor in some continuation of our lives after death? Such a 'when' question cannot be answered, since we cannot apply to eternity concepts of time. It is simply not possible either to describe or to imagine how this 'consummation' and 'fulfilment' take place. Rahner's elusiveness here can be irritating, but he would argue that it is in fact quite proper. It is part of our human situation that we go towards death as towards the unknown, that we are not in control of our destination, that we have no map with which to make sense of it all. We can hope, Rahner would say, for the fulfilment of our lives in eternity, in part because we already have had some glimpses of eternity (for instance, in our sense of absolute responsibility), but this does not mean that we know exactly how it all works. Our lack of understanding is appropriate and indeed biblical. The Bible gives us a host of images but no particularly clear map of what is to come:

> Scripture describes the content of the blessed life of the dead in a thousand images: as rest and peace, as a banquet and as glory, as being at home in the Father's house, as the kingdom of God's eternal Lordship, as the community of all who have reached blessed fulfilment, as the inheritance of God's glory, as a day which will never end, and as satisfaction without boredom. Throughout all of the words of scripture we always surmise one and the same thing: God is absolute mystery. And therefore fulfilment and absolute closeness to God himself is also an ineffable mystery . . . (FCF 441)

Criticism in the Church

What is the role of Roman Catholic theologians when the church authorities make a pronouncement – a pronouncement on, say, birth control or the ordination of women or the absolute nature of morality? One quite common view, and one which has been voiced by some recent popes, is that whatever the theologians' private opinions may previously have been, their job is to accept the teaching of Rome and do their best to provide intellectual support for it, both by explaining its meaning and by developing arguments to justify it. Rahner rejects this view. Even when the Church teaches with authority, Rahner maintains, the theologian almost always remains free to voice criticism.

Rahner holds that in general criticism plays an important role in the Church, and that it is something which is not only allowed, but required:

> the Church's self-understanding and its own faith do not merely permit the Catholic to have an oppositional relationship to the Church . . . or make this unavoidable. An attitude of this kind is actually required of us. (TI XVII 129)

Catholics not only *may* criticize the Church, but they *must* do so, for the Church, like its members, is sinful and always in need of reform.

Criticism from within the Church, however, differs from attack from without. Internal criticism, Rahner writes, 'must rest on the basis of an ultimate assent to the Church's message and its self-understanding' and it must respect 'the faith of the Church, its permanent identity and its historical continuity' (TI XVII 131). One criticizes on the basis of a deeper acceptance.

Internal critics, furthermore, must be careful. They must also be self-critical; they must remember that they too are sinners and play some part in the sinfulness of the Church. In an interview broadcast as part of a series called 'The Angry Old Men', Rahner spoke with irritation of critics who

> behave as if they're especially wise and holy, and suffer the most from the Church's defects and failings to which they haven't contributed in any way. (KRD 331)

Criticism within the Church, Rahner thinks, ought to have a particular tone:

> Criticism should only be spoken or written when critics are in a good mood, when they can laugh and show loving good will to those they criticize, when they know that those they criticize are also not geniuses or saints, but on

closer examination are as lovable, friendly and reasonable as the critics consider themselves to be. (KRD 331)

Of the many kinds of criticism which go on in the Church, one is the criticism of official teachings coming from those in positions of authority. Such criticism is possible, according to Rahner, because what is owed to official teaching is not unquestioning acceptance, but a recognition of and respect for the particular weight of authority attached to a given pronouncement, and such respect is usually (though not quite always) compatible with critical questioning.

In very rare cases a teaching may count as 'infallible': according to the understanding of the Catholic Church, such a teaching cannot be false. And in such cases, Rahner believes, the theologian cannot question the truth of the pronouncement and remain within the Church. But even this is not quite as restrictive as it might seem. Although one cannot question the truth of an infallible statement, one can doubt whether making such a statement was necessary or appropriate, and one can investigate the *meaning* of the statement. So, for example, during Rahner's lifetime there was only one instance of an infallible declaration: in 1950 Pope Pius XII defined as doctrine the proposition that Mary was assumed, body and soul, into heaven. Rahner as a loyal Catholic theologian does not dispute the truth of this statement, but he has a particular understanding of how it ought to be understood. It becomes, under his interpretation, on the one hand something which follows from more general principles (a proper understanding of Mary as 'radically redeemed', and a proper understanding of Jesus' resurrection), and on the other hand something which is not especially shocking or magical. On his interpretation, the doctrine of the Assumption simply tells us that Mary can be known to be among those (and there must be some, since human nature is intrinsically social) who even now are with Jesus, existing in a state of perfection.

All other official pronouncements – all non-infallible pronouncements – may be wrong. This does not mean that they
necessarily *are* wrong, or that they should be dismissed or
ignored or treated as just one more statement of opinion among
many. They do still carry varying degrees of authority, and must
accordingly be respected and taken seriously. But they are nevertheless open to question and to criticism. How does this work?
How can one simultaneously respect a teaching and criticize
it? The easiest way to see what Rahner understands by all this is
to look at his own response to authoritative teachings, and in
particular his response to a teaching on contraception issued
in the 1960s, and to a declaration on the ordination of women
from the 1970s.

In 1968 Pope Paul VI threw the Catholic Church into turmoil
by issuing *Humanae Vitae*, an encyclical (official letter) which
included, and has come to be known for, a condemnation of
artificial birth control. Rahner's comments on it are very deli-
cately balanced. On the one hand, he maintains that Catholics
must take the encyclical seriously, and be prepared to rethink
their own positions in the light of it. *Humanae Vitae*

> is the pronouncement of a pope. It is certainly the out-
> come of mature thought and preparation. In the Catholic
> Church it has a notable doctrinal tradition behind it.
> Under these circumstances it is meaningless and contrary
> to the seriousness with which the question should be
> taken, and the respect due to the authority of the pope,
> if our reactions to the encyclical simply take the form of
> short-sighted emotionalism; if all we can do is to produce
> crude and distorted summaries of its contents, and to
> ascribe to the pope motives which are designed to render
> his pronouncements unworthy of belief from the outset.
> Anyone who from the outset maintains his own opinion
> as indisputable without any self-criticism . . . cannot, as a
> Catholic, do justice to the encyclical. (TI XI 264)

On the other hand, he points out that *Humanae Vitae* makes no infallible pronouncements, that it is in principle revisable, and that history gives us plenty of examples of papal teachings of a similar status which have in fact turned out to be wrong. In view of the authority of the encyclical there should be a presumption in its favour, then, but in view of its fallibility this is a presumption which can be overridden.

Rahner is rather cautious and avoids actually taking a position on whether *Humanae Vitae* is right or wrong. What he argues, however, is that even if one assumes that it is right, the case against it is sufficiently strong, and the whole situation sufficiently difficult, that one should expect large numbers of Catholics to reject it *in good conscience*. Though there may be a presumption that *Humanae Vitae* is right, there should also be a presumption that those who reject it and use artificial contraception are acting in accordance with their conscience. Their decision should be respected, and they should not be made to feel guilty, or treated as 'bad Catholics'.

In 1976 the Sacred Congregation for the Doctrine of the Faith (the modern successor to the Inquisition) published a document which denied the possibility of the Catholic Church ordaining women: it maintained that there is a constant tradition in the Church excluding women from ordination, that Jesus and the Apostles deliberately excluded women, and that therefore the Church has no power to ordain women. In response to this document Rahner shows somewhat less caution than in his comments on *Humanae Vitae*. He begins by acknowledging that the theologian owes a certain respect to the document as 'an authentic declaration of the Roman authorities on faith' (TI XX 37), but he goes on to attack its arguments at every point. The 'constant tradition' in the Church is no guarantee of anything, for there can be merely human traditions in the Church, and there have in the past been long-standing traditions which were eventually rejected (condoning slavery, for instance, and forbidding the charging of interest). The document makes a too simple jump from the idea of apostles, and 'the Twelve' whom Jesus chose, to the idea of priests. It fails to consider the fact that neither Jesus nor the Apostles, all of whom expected the imminent end of the world, were likely to have been working out plans for the long-term future of the Church. And above all it fails to make the case that in excluding women from certain roles Jesus and the Apostles were acting independently of all cultural conditioning.

How can one say a document is faulty at every point and still respect it? Rahner suggests that the theologian's respect for such a declaration consists in three things. First of all, one does one's best to appreciate its arguments (which may nevertheless turn out to be unpersuasive). Secondly, one accepts that practically speaking it is for the moment binding – one cannot for the present go around ordaining women. And thirdly, one takes it as an indication that the Church is in any case not yet ready to think of ordaining women.

Desire

Rahner has an unusual ability to breathe fresh life into ancient theological notions, and his treatment of the concept of concupiscence provides an example of this. Since the time of St Augustine concupiscence has been understood to be one of the results of 'the Fall', a consequence of original sin. It refers to desires which spring up in all human beings, outside of their conscious control. We are not absolute masters of ourselves: even if we manage not to act upon our desires, we cannot simply banish them. The traditional understanding has been that the desires in question are desires associated with the senses: it is a matter of the lower, sense-bound part of the human being rebelling against the higher, 'spiritual' part. And like the word 'desire' itself, concupiscence carries particular sexual overtones (though in principle it would also include, say, an immoderate urge to eat chocolate). Theologians have been divided over the question of how exactly to classify concupiscence: the great Protestant thinkers have considered it in itself to be an offence against God and therefore intrinsically sinful, whereas Roman Catholicism has insisted since the Council of Trent (1545–63) that although concupiscence arises from sin, and tends to lead to sin, it is not in itself sinful. All sides have agreed, in any case, that it is a nasty and regrettable business.

Rahner makes two objections to the usual understanding of concupiscence. For a variety of reasons, first of all, he thinks it a mistake to associate concupiscence only with the supposedly lower, sensual part of the human being. We can sin, or be tempted to sin, on the 'spiritual' level also – and Rahner suggests in any case that these two aspects of a human being cannot be so neatly separated. Secondly, spontaneous and involuntary desires can lead us either towards evil or towards good, and Rahner claims that it makes no sense to label as concupiscence only the desires which tend towards wrong-doing. The argument that he makes for this point is a technical one, but what emerges is a new and rather interesting concept of concupiscence.

Concupiscence should be understood, Rahner proposes, simply as the resistance from within us that our freedom meets. Freedom, as Rahner understands it, is most fundamentally the freedom to be who we choose to be. We also have a certain freedom, of course, to make choices about external things, but in making such choices we are always at the same time determining something about ourselves, and this Rahner takes to be the key element. Freedom is essentially freedom over ourselves. But we are not in fact in full control of ourselves. We do not fully and immediately *become* our choices. And this is the meaning of concupiscence. We cannot simply gather ourselves up and commit ourselves utterly in one particular direction, for we always meet some resistance and inertia. We are to one degree or another at odds with ourselves. We can firmly decide to be brave, and then tremble; we can lie, and then give ourselves away with a blush. We make a decision, but we are unable to bring the whole of ourselves along with us. Human beings are not wholly *integrated* beings.

This lack of integration works both for us and against us. It is because of it that when we sin and turn from God, we do not automatically become fixed for ever in an evil course (as, for instance, fallen angels are traditionally presumed to do). Concupiscence on this understanding can protect us from ourselves: it prevents us from ever becoming, in Rahner's phrase, 'wholly absorbed' in evil. On the other hand, it also means that the Christian life has to be one long struggle, not just against 'the desires of the flesh' but against all that is in the person that cannot immediately and automatically be brought into harmony with the fundamental, basic decision to accept God's grace. Progress in the Christian life, then, is not a matter of a change in one's most fundamental commitment, but of an increasing integration of the whole of one's nature with this fundamental commitment, and only to the degree that this is accomplished and concupiscence overcome (something which never happens fully in this life) can we love God with our 'whole heart'. What Rahner does, then, is to take a tradition of thought about spontaneous impulses and involuntary desires, and place it in a dramatically new context. He frees the notion of concupiscence from the usual narrowly sexual connotations, and uses it to characterize a fundamental feature of human nature.

8

Rahner the man

Those who write about the grand themes of God, Christ and humanity, faith, hope and love, leave us wondering about their own relation to God, the quality of their own humanity, the nature of their own faith. Out of what sort of a person do these thoughts come? Whether the thinker should matter, or only the thought itself, is something that can be debated, but in any case we cannot help but be interested in the personality lying behind the writings.

Rahner was not terribly forthcoming about himself. He refused to write an autobiography or to publish memoirs. He gave quite a few interviews, but used them for the most part to talk about theology and the state of the Church rather than about himself. When pressed he did his best to make his life sound as uninteresting as possible. He grew up in a 'normal, middle-class, Christian family', or more precisely, 'middle- to lower-middle class' (IR 24). He was one of seven children: 'Naturally we loved each other, if one wants to use this pompous word. But in those days there were few problems; at most the kind that everyone has' (IR 31). During his school years he was 'an average pupil who found classes somewhat boring'.

Again and again one finds Rahner refusing to portray himself or his life in any sort of dramatic terms. Asked what motivated him to become a Jesuit, his reply was

Well, I must say that I actually can't give you any special information about that. Sometime ask an average man, married some fifty or sixty years, what really prompted him to marry this particular Maria Meier. If he doesn't fib or hasn't lived a life of intense self-reflection, he's likely to say: 'I completely admit the fact that I did that. I was faithful to my decision and was happy throughout the fifty or sixty years of my marriage. I also accept the fact that normal human motivations prompted my decision. But I cannot give you any more exact psychological information.'

I have to say the same thing about my Jesuit vocation. Obviously I could tell you what might prompt a reasonable young man to become a priest or a Jesuit, and what it might mean to assume the priestly ministry in such a tightly knit and organized society rather than as a diocesan priest. But then these are all such general and obvious motives that they say very little about my own case. (IR 35)

What was it like in the middle of his theological career, Rahner was asked, when he was partially silenced, and threatened with a censor? Nothing special, really:

I would say that all the things that happened did not affect me as terribly as they might affect young theologians today. You see, if a person is a member of a religious order, a Jesuit, and really takes into account the fact that his religious superior can send him to India or to the African bush – and that this can happen without further ado – then one does not get so frightfully worked up about getting into occasional difficulties with Rome over one's theological work.

When the Congregation of Faith in Rome under Cardinal Ottaviani once said that I could write only in conjunction with a special Roman censor, then I said to myself: 'Well, I just won't write any more, and then the matter is over and done with, right?'[1] (IR 63)

Again, when asked about the extraordinary quantity of his writings, Rahner insisted there was nothing really interesting or unusual in it – he had few hobbies, he did not lead an intense social life, and the work came naturally.

Rahner's reticence may be a product of a naturally taciturn character (his school religion teacher suggested he should not become a Jesuit because he was too 'withdrawn and grumpy') or of a desire to thwart the attempts of interviewers and others to romanticize him as a 'great man', or both. But in any case it has not been mirrored by his friends and students, who speak and write of him with real enthusiasm. He was a charismatic lecturer, and a man who inspired loyalty and affection among those who knew him. One learns from these of a love of ice cream, fast cars and aeroplanes, of a fascination with engineering and toy shops, of a consistent charm and hospitality towards visitors, and of a variety of rather surprising good deeds (for instance, bringing bags of groceries to a widow or typing the thesis of a student in trouble). And finally, friends and admirers insist on an unusual degree of integration between Rahner's own spirituality and his theological work.

What emerges from Rahner's own writings, from interviews, and from the reminiscences of others is altogether a rather appealing character – grumpy but charming.[2] Rahner admittedly does not cut a particularly heroic figure compared to, say, Dietrich Bonhoeffer, a Lutheran theologian executed by the Nazis for plotting against Hitler. And yet his unheroic, quiet, hard-working life is somehow in keeping with his theology and its insistence on the encounter with God in the day-to-day duties and experiences of life.

A good place to end is perhaps with Rahner's own attempt, three years before his death, to encapsulate the flavour of his life and its significance.

... my life has been, at bottom, a very prosaic affair. Nothing very exciting happened; in general, one just tried to do (at least) one's duty as well as possible; there weren't any spectacular peaks. That is how it should be. As with a woman who takes in laundry and brings up her children and has to wait and see if they turn out well or not, until it is over for her. Something like this seems to me to be the normal life for most of us and this too is what my life has been like.

I never had terrible diseases; I came through two world wars in an almost indecently untroubled fashion; I never came close to starvation. No particularly dramatic things happened in my life as a Jesuit and priest, either. I never had the slightest inclination to write memoirs, an autobiography, or Confessions in the manner of Augustine.

A year ago in March I had a private audience with Pope John Paul II. I knew him already from Cracow. He started out by inquiring how things were going. I said in German: 'I am retired, living in Munich, and waiting to die.' Perhaps it took him back a bit. But what I said was accurate. I have managed to live the life of a schoolmaster, without either heroic high points or terrible trials. That is something I cannot do anything about; it simply happened that way and I have accepted it. How does Goethe put it, 'dreary weeks, cheerful feasts'? I have, of course, had my share of that too.

One's personal life is nobody else's business. What I have to say, therefore, is only: Accept the moment. See to it that you do what one can call, without any folderol, your duty. All the same, be ready again and again to realize once more, that the ineffable mystery we call God not only lives and reigns, but had the unlikely idea to approach you personally in love; turn your eyes to Jesus, the crucified one; come what may, you will be able to accept your life from him when all is said and done. I cannot really say more than these well-worn Christian platitudes. I wonder how much longer it will last before night falls for ever.

I do not know. You go on as long as daylight lasts. In the end you leave with empty hands, that I know; and it is well. At that moment you look at the crucified one and go. What comes is the everlasting mystery of God. (KRD 275)

A guide to further reading

The largest collection of Rahner's writings is contained in the 23 volumes of the *Theological Investigations*. These cover a tremendous variety of topics, from angels to nuclear weapons to the experience of God to the history of the sacrament of penance, and they make for interesting browsing. The essays in the final volumes tend to be shorter, simpler and more accessible; the most difficult and also the richest pieces are found in some of the early volumes.

The Practice of Faith, edited by Karl Lehmann and Albert Raffelt, is a very useful single-volume collection of Rahner's writings. It is a rich and wide-ranging compilation of fairly brief (1–10 pages) extracts from Rahner's pastoral and spiritual works. Since Rahner's academic theology and his spiritual writings are closely intertwined, much that is at the heart of his thought is touched on here.

One way to begin reading Rahner is by way of his writings on prayer, for instance *Encounters with Silence* or *On Prayer*. Another possibility is to start by reading transcripts of interviews he gave. The most useful collection of these is *Karl Rahner in Dialogue*. *Faith in a Wintry Season*, containing interviews he gave in the last two years before his death, is also interesting, as is the autobiographical interview *I Remember*.

Rahner's most systematic work is *Foundations of Christian Faith: An Introduction to the Idea of Christianity*. In spite of the subtitle, this is a difficult book which does *not* make a good introduction to Rahner's thought, and is best avoided initially.

It is easier to get a feeling for Rahner by browsing through the many and varied essays of the *Theological Investigations* than by trying to swallow him whole in the *Foundations of Christian Faith.*

Those particularly interested in the philosophical side of Rahner's thought might want to look at *Hearer of the Word*, originally a set of lectures on the philosophy of religion, or *Spirit in the World*, originally Rahner's (failed) doctoral thesis in philosophy. Both works are difficult. Of the two *Hearer of the Word* is slightly more accessible, particularly in the recently published translation by Joseph Donceel.

Rahner wrote a great deal more than can be mentioned here. A bibliography of what is available in English can be found in Volume 25 of *The Heythrop Journal.*

Notes

Introduction

1 With the Second Vatican Council came the effective end of neo-scholasticism. Rahner and others of his generation, one might say, had been so successful in 'opening up' the system that the system in fact ceased to exist.

2 Rahner was not alone in his efforts to open up neo-scholasticism. In fact his interpretation of Aquinas draws heavily on the work of a Belgian Jesuit philosopher of the previous generation, Joseph Maréchal.

1   God and humanity

1 *Spirit in the World* is an interpretation of the 'metaphysics of knowledge' of Thomas Aquinas in the light of modern philosophy, in the course of which Rahner develops his own rather technical philosophical arguments. It was originally a Ph.D. thesis in philosophy, but was failed by Rahner's supervisor, Martin Honecker, a somewhat more traditional reader of Aquinas.

2 Rahner sometimes writes of a 'mediated immediacy' to God. Our relation to God is mediated because there is always some finite object involved. But the relation to God is nevertheless an immediate one in the sense that the object does not come *between* us and God – it does not cause us to meet God at second hand.

3 It must be said that Rahner is a little vague about what precisely can count as the articulation of transcendental experience. Often he suggests something along the lines of the list cited, but when it suits his purposes he seems willing to call anything whatsoever within the realm of categorical experience an expression, or attempted expression, of transcendental experience.

2   Christ and grace

1 This is a formula that can, it should be noted, be reversed: if we really take Christ seriously, we can allow even our thinking about ourselves to be shaped by what we learn from him.

2 There is no need, of course, to think that Rahner makes use of a *prior* conception of what humanity is to interpret Christ. One can at least as legitimately see the whole vision of human nature I described in the last chapter as already shaped by Christology.

3 This analogy does nothing to support the idea that the incarnation happens only once, of course, since there are a number of people capable of these mathematical feats. On the other hand, Rahner is not claiming to *prove* from first principles the Christian belief that the incarnation happened, and happened only once, but merely trying to *make sense* of this belief. For a more complex defence of Rahner's Christology see Philip Endean's 'Rahner, Christology and Grace', *The Heythrop Journal* XXXVI (1996) 284–97.

4 Rahner's concept of grace is itself arguably derived from Christology, so once again it needs to be stressed that it is not a matter here of imposing some *prior* conception of grace or God's relation to the world upon Christology.

5 How, one might ask, does speaking of grace as a communication rather than simply as a gift advance our understanding of it? The short answer is probably that it does not. What it does, however, is to allow Rahner to build a very close link between ideas of grace and ideas of revelation.

6 Karl Barth, *The Word of God and the Word of Man* (London: Hodder 8 Stoughton, 1928), 196.

4   Sacraments and symbols

1 Rahner would perhaps respond that the concept, because it is so basic, is inherently flexible.

2 This claim can only work because, as we saw in the previous chapter, Rahner has a rather slippery way of using the notion of 'Church'.

5   Philosophy and Rahner's theology

1 From the preface to Louis Roberts, *The Achievement of Karl Rahner* (New York: Herder & Herder, 1967).

2 Paul Imhof and Hubert Biallowuns, eds, *Faith in a Wintry Season: Conversations and Interviews with Karl Rahner in the Last Years of His Life* (New York: Crossroad, 1991), 22.

3 In *Karl Rahner: Theology and Philosophy* (London: Routledge, 2004).

4 Again, the interested reader might like to look at my *Karl Rahner: Theology and Philosophy* for a more comprehensive treatment of his intervention here, including a treatment of *changes* in Rahner's views. Here I am presenting a rather simplified account.

5 Cf. *Karl Rahner: Theology and Philosophy*, 22–31.

6   Spirituality and Rahner's theology

1 The title of this prayer has been translated 'God of My Daily Routine' or 'God of My Daily Drudge'. For the latter translation, see Philip Endean, ed., *Karl Rahner: Spiritual Writings* (Maryknoll, NY: Orbis, 2004).

2 Interestingly, drabness, pettiness and boredom are much more likely to make an appearance in Rahner's writing than vivid and dramatic evil.

3 Ignatius, *Spiritual Exercises*, n.34.5–7, quoted in Philip Endean, *Karl Rahner and Ignatian Spirituality* (Oxford: Oxford University Press, 2001), 18.

4 *Karl Rahner and Ignatian Spirituality*, 7.

5 This is not intended as a criticism of Endean, whose argument I have dramatically oversimplified here.

8   Rahner the man

1 Rahner makes it clear that this sort of remark is not meant to condone the methods Rome was using:

> . . . things happened time and again that as far as the Romans are concerned are more or less self-evident practices and ways of looking at things. They are things that I have absolutely no wish to defend when I say that I did not personally feel so terribly persecuted. You've got to distinguish between how an old-style theologian like myself experiences things like that and the totally different question of how the objective procedures of the Congregation of Faith ought to be conducted.

They must be just, therefore objective, and the greatest stupidities must not be allowed to occur. (IR 66)

2 The phrase 'grumpy charm' comes originally from Mario von Galli, and is quoted by one of Rahner's interviewers, Meinhold Krauss.

Index